CHALLENGES TO PEACE IN THE MIDDLE EAST

CHALLENGES TO PEACE IN THE MIDDLE EAST

DENNIS G. STEVENS

LAKE ERIE COLLEGE

New York   San Francisco   Boston
London   Toronto   Sydney   Tokyo   Singapore   Madrid
Mexico City   Munich   Paris   Cape Town   Hong Kong   Montreal

Vice President/Publisher: Priscilla McGeehon
Executive Editor: Eric Stano
Senior Marketing Manager: Megan Galvin-Fak
Production Manager: Denise Phillip
Project Coordination, Text Design, and Electronic Page Makeup: WestWords, Inc.
Cover Design Manager: John Callahan
Cover Design: Kay Petronio
Cover Photo: © David Lees/CORBIS
Senior Manufacturing Buyer: Dennis J. Para
Printer and Binder: Courier Corporation
Cover Printer: Lehigh Press, Inc.

Library of Congress Cataloging-in-Publication Data

Stevens, Dennis G.
    Challenges to peace in the Middle East / Dennis G. Stevens.
        p. cm.
    Includes bibliographical references and index.
    ISBN 0-205-28063-3
    1. Middle East—Relations—United States. 2. United States—Relations—
    Middle East. 3. Arab-Israeli conflict—1993—Peace 4. Nationalism—Middle
    East. I. Title.

DS63.2.U5 S72 2002
956.05'4—dc21

                                                                2002034129

Please visit our website at http://www.ablongman.com

ISBN 0-205-28063-3

2 3 4 5 6 7 8 9 10—CRS—05 04 03

To
my parents, Richard and Norma Stevens,
with love and respect

Brief Contents

Detailed Contents

Preface

The war on terrorism declared by President George W. Bush after the September 11th, 2001 attacks on New York and Washington thrust Iraq into the center of events in the Middle East.

Within a year of the attacks, Bush had moved from his focus on Afghanistan and the Al-Qaida organization, which he held directly responsible for the attacks, to a broader interest in regimes like Iraq that supported terrorism and were developing weapons of mass destruction. Even though some critics in Congress thought that this development revealed a lack of clarity about administration goals, Bush declared Saddam Hussein a threat to world peace and called for a "regime change" in Iraq.

By the summer of 2002, the American military seemed to be planning a full-scale invasion of Iraq, and Congress began a debate over a resolution granting Bush the power to use any means necessary, including force, to remove Saddam Hussein from power. As Bush attempted to focus world attention on Iraq, tensions between the Israelis and Palestinians increased; suicide bombers attacked civilians in Israel with alarming frequency, and Israel—holding Arafat largely responsible for the attacks—used political and military force to attempt to drive him from office. The peace that so many had thought was so close after the Gulf War and the Oslo Accords had disappeared.

This book attempts to examine the question of why peace seems so difficult to achieve in the Middle East. It does not offer a comprehensive history of the region or encyclopedic profiles of countries; rather, it offers a short introduction to the Middle East by examining a number of challenges to peace. Its argument is that the problems of the Middle East are particularly difficult to resolve because they are layered, with one problem or issue lying on top of another.

For example, disagreements between the Israelis and the Syrians over the Golan Heights in some ways reflect current political and economic realities, but the disagreements also have to be understood in the context of the legacy of European imperialism, since the boundaries of both countries were drawn European powers. But European imperialism is not entirely to blame here. The Ottoman Empire controlled the region before the Europeans, and their control involved tax and land policies that influenced the development of the area. The conflict also rests on conflicting aspirations of Arab and Jewish nationalism, and these conflicting versions of nationalism are not entirely independent of religious and ethnic differences.

While it is true that one will encounter complexities in every area of study and in every part of the world, the Middle East seems to be a place where the layering of issues is especially important. Another way of explaining this is to say that in the Middle East, the past imposes itself upon the present in a particularly aggressive manner. This book suggests that students of the Middle East have to follow the example of archeologists who need to strip away layer after layer of earth in order to uncover the truth they seek.

The idea for this book took form over the last ten years as I taught a Middle East course to undergraduates. I searched for but was unable to find a short introduction to the Middle East that I could assign to my students that still allowed me the time to examine in depth a select number of timely and important topics. Most introductory texts were too long and covered topics that my students weren't really ready to address. One should be able to use this book and still devote a significant amount of attention to other issues one considers to be important, such as modernization, Islamic revivalism, or political development.

By focusing on conflict and the problems standing in the way of resolving conflict, this book does not mean to suggest that the Middle East can be understood completely in terms of conflict. No single issue defines the Middle East. But since this is the issue that often first attracts students to the study of the Middle East, it seemed to be a useful topic for organizing the book.

This book is unique in that it begins with an analysis of American perceptions of the Middle East. Part One is devoted to three areas where common American perceptions stand in the way of understanding. Many Americans believe that the oil-producing countries are rich and powerful and exert a sinister influence on world affairs. Chapter One attempts to show that oil wealth has actually been a mixed blessing in the Middle East.

Chapter Two looks at the influence that the Gulf War has had on American sensibilities. This should be especially relevant at a time when another Gulf War is a strong possibility. Chapter Three addresses an issue that no other introductory text on the market has dealt with seriously: stereotypes of Muslims and Jews. These stereotypes are important because they affect the way in which Americans relate to Muslims and Jews in general, and they are important because they influence the way foreign policy in the United States is developed and legitimized.

Part Two examines the way in which history lives in contemporary events. Chapter Four introduces the general topic of imperialism and suggests that today's politics are influenced by the memories of European intervention through the Mandate period. Chapters Five and Six focus on Arab and Jewish nationalism. Many of the current disagreements between Israelis and Palestinians can be understood more fully once the origins of these movements are clarified. Chapter Seven offers a short history of what was once known as the Arab-Israeli conflict and is now known as the Israeli-Palestinian conflict.

Part Three of the book looks at the changes that have taken place in the Middle East. Chapter Eight looks at the tension between tradition and modernization by focusing on the case of Iran. It also introduces the topic of political reform by examining the drive for democratization in Jordan and Kuwait. Chapter Nine addresses the issue of terrorism by examining three forms of terrorism: religiously motivated terrorism, politically motivated terrorism, and state-sponsored terrorism. Finally, Chapter Ten looks at the growing disillusionment in the Peace Process. After what many people considered to be a promising beginning in 1993 with the Oslo Accords, the Peace Process seems stalled. Not only has the violence continued, but serious negotiations seem completely abandoned. This chapter considers two perspectives on the Peace Process. Could the problem be that the Palestinians do not really want peace, or could the problem be that the Israelis do not, in fact, want peace? A growing number of people subscribe to one of these views. In any case, peace will be difficult to achieve until this issue is resolved. A commitment to the possibility of peace does not, in itself, produce peace, but progress toward peace is not possible without it.

ACKNOWLEDGMENTS

Many people have contributed to this book, some in ways that are evident and can be explained easily, and others in more subtle, indirect ways. Some contributions to this book cannot be acknowledged enough, and some cannot be acknowledged at all. I would like to thank Eric Stano, Executive Editor of Political Science at Longman, for his tireless and generous attention. I am indebted to Patrick Burt and Julie Hollist of WestWords for the thorough and thoughtful editing they did. The book is significantly better than it would have been because of their work. I am also grateful to the comments and suggestions from Edward L. Angus of Fort Lewis College, Jim Brown of Central Washington University, David A. Cowell of Drew University, W. Martin James of Henderson State University, Christopher M. Jones of Northern Illinois University, Charles Lindholm of Boston University, Sharon Murphy of Nazareth College of Rochester, Adam L. Silverman of the University of Florida and William James Stover of Santa Clara University.

Special thanks have to go to colleagues and friends such as Peter Schotten, Jim Meader, Joe Dondelinger, and Charles Azzara for their substantive advice and their encouragement. I am grateful to Augustana College for the two research grants it made available to support work on the book. And I cannot possibly think of a way to thank my family enough. My daughters Sarah and Rachel were a constant comfort. My wife, Bonnie, helped me every day in ways she cannot know, and she taught me to think clearly and deeply about the Middle East. I am grateful to all of these people for helping me through the complex process of thinking and working that culminated in the writing of this book.

Introduction

In spite of the seemingly endless efforts of diplomats and heads of state, in spite of the contributions of international organizations, and in spite of the loving work of ordinary people uniting to increase understanding and communication, peace in the Middle East remains elusive. This book explores what can best be described as challenges to peace in the Middle East, from the legacy of imperialism to the introduction of new tensions by international terrorism. In other words, it attempts to provide an introduction to the problems and issues that stand in the way of any serious resolution of tensions in the region.

Because of the centrality of the dispute between Israel and the Palestinians to the Middle East, special attention will be devoted to it. The contention of this book is that the problems of the Middle East are particularly difficult to understand because they do not exist in isolation; they are layered on top of one another. Every time one issue is examined, another issue emerges that must be studied before the first can be understood thoroughly. The next issue leads to another, and the process continues with new complexities continually asserting themselves. While it is true that in any area of study one will encounter complexities, the Middle East seems to be one place where the layering of issues is particularly significant, where the past imposes itself upon the present.

In a sense, one must approach the Middle East as an archeologist would, gently exploring the earth and stripping away layer after layer in order to discover the facts and to see how they relate to one another. In the end, some uncertainty always remains about whether one has really found the truth. Have time and the elements hidden the facts? Or has the archeologist approached his or her subject dogmatically, imposing his or her view of the world on the facts in such a way as to distort them and actually to erect barriers to understanding? Even the dominant theories and perspectives in the scholarly world can turn out to be nothing more than bias cloaked with academic language.

LANGUAGE

So how does one begin to study a subject as complex as the Middle East? The first issue that must be addressed is language. Many languages are spoken in the Middle East, but the most important for the purposes of this book is Arabic. Since Arabic does not use the English alphabet, variant spellings of Arabic words are common in English. This text follows the approach to transliteration in the *International Journal of Middle East Studies*, but be aware that as you begin to read widely in the field of Middle Eastern studies, words that are familiar to you may be spelled in unfamiliar ways.

Words used to define an area of study sometimes reflect a particular perspective or interpretation of the subject itself. Consider the debate over abortion. If one uses the term "unborn child" in the debate, the implication is that abortion is wrong because it involves taking a meaningful, human life. If, on the other hand, one uses the term "fetus," one suggests that while potential life may exist, abortion is actually a medical procedure that does not terminate a meaningful, human life and that women can therefore make the abortion decision themselves. The terms of the debate actually narrow the possibilities for true inquiry.

The same is true of the Middle East. There are a number of words that conjure up deceptive images that stand in the way of clarity in study. For example, the word *jihad* is often misused. It is often translated as "holy war," and suggests that Muslims are violent and extreme in their perspective on life and in their actions. To some the word suggests that Islam and terrorism are the same. The word actually means "struggle," and refers first and foremost to the struggle of the individual for purity and goodness of the soul. The word can also be used in a political context to refer to the necessity of defending the religion or a country that honors Islam from its enemies. There is nothing frightening or unusual in this attitude. Both Judaism and Christianity recognize that self-defense is sometimes necessary. The concept of *jihad* can be expanded in disturbing ways by those who wish to use the word to promote their political agendas, but any concept in any religion can be abused.

Expressions designed to define political activity can also be presented in a misleading manner. The words "militant" and "protester" are used—often without any justification—to describe individuals or groups in order to promote a political perspective. If someone is a "militant," he or she is not only dangerous, but is involved in what is probably illegitimate political activity. On the other hand, if someone is a "protester," then he or she is simply attempting to register a claim of justice against a more powerful opponent. The tradition of political speech in the West stigmatizes militancy and legitimizes protest.

Other terms are also used in problematic ways. For example, "left wing" and "right wing" are used in the West to apply to extremist perspectives. In the United States, for example, Democrats and Republicans are considered mainstream political groups, but anarchists are "left wing" and neo-Nazis are "right wing." These are useful political terms, but they can be used to attack political opponents by denying that they fit within mainstream politics. It is much too easy to use these convenient political terms to create a misleading picture of politics in the Middle East. The moment someone is identified as "left wing" or "right wing" that person is presented as an extremist of some sort. It would be misleading, for example, to label the Labor Party in Israel as a "left wing" organization or to label the Likud Party as "right wing," although the Labor Party might include some people who could rightly be described as "left wing" and the Likud Party might include some people who could rightly be described as "right wing." Both groups, however, exist within mainstream politics in the Middle East, even if they are unfamiliar to many in the West.

The phrase "Muslim Fundamentalism" is also misleading. Fundamentalists are those who return to what they believe is a pure or literal understanding of their sacred texts and then base their lives in an uncompromising way on that understanding. The term probably came into existence in the twentieth century as a way for Christians to define new protestant movements in the United States. In some ways it seems convenient to take a familiar term like "fundamentalism" and apply it to an unfamiliar phenomenon with the hope that it will aid understanding. But many Muslims reject the idea that those referred to as Muslim Fundamentalists are really returning to the roots of their religion. In many ways, the groups often identified as Muslim Fundamentalists have developed new ideas that depart from tradition. In particular, the Fundamentalist belief that the state as a governmental entity must be ruled by *sharia,* or Islamic law, reveals that these groups are accepting the modern nation-state as the foundation of their views.[1] It is important to recognize that those called Muslim Fundamentalists disagree with one another about basic issues of faith and action; the term is at the very least too vague. Whether or not one accepts the notion that Muslim Fundamentalists accurately represent traditional Islam, it should at least be clear that the term should not be applied to terrorist groups. In the Western press, a Muslim Fundamentalist is a murderer who is devoted to the destruction of the United States, but Islam does not sanction the murder of innocent people.

GEOGRAPHY

What is the Middle East? The term itself is problematic. It was invented in 1902 by an American naval historian Alfred Mahan to describe the area between Arabia and India from the military perspective of a time when European foreign policy defined much of the world. Since its creation, it has come to be used by almost everyone, even though it is now used to describe a much larger area than was

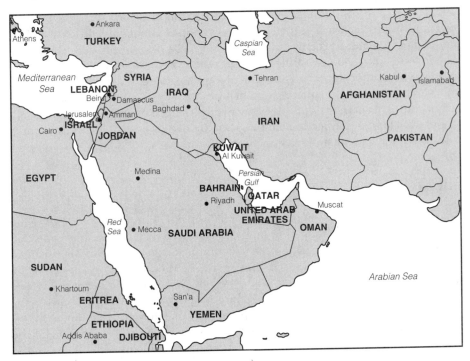

Figure 1 The Middle East

originally intended. What exactly is comprised by the Middle East? It describes at the bare minimum an uncertain but large area that includes countries from Egypt in the west to Turkey and Iran in the east. Some include countries south of Egypt such as the Sudan and Ethiopia, and most include countries west of Egypt such as Lybia, Algeria, and Morocco. Does the Middle East include countries east of Iran such as Afghanistan and Pakistan? Perhaps. This is all a matter of dispute, but in spite of the problems with the term, almost everyone has accepted it for the sake of convenience. Since the term was not coined by the people of the region, its meaning must always remain somewhat vague. It is probably more important for students to gain some familiarity with the region than to accept a particular definition of the Middle East. One should pay attention to where countries are in relation to one another. These relationships are more important than shifting labels.

The same is true for the term "Palestine." It does not appear in the Hebrew or Christian Scriptures; Jews and early Christians spoke first of Israel, and then later of the division of Israel into two kingdoms, the northern kingdom of Judah (the word "Jew" means people of Judah) and the southern kingdom of Israel. After the Romans destroyed the Jewish Temple in the year 70 A.D., the term Palestine (meaning the land of the Philistines) was commonly substituted for Judah and Israel as a way of eliminating what was for the Romans a troublesome Jewish identity. The word Palestine continued to be used through the time of the Ottoman Empire, although it designated a general area rather than a specific country. By the time the French and English began to pay attention to the Middle East in order to advance their imperial interests, Palestine included what is today Israel and Jordan, as well as parts of what are now Lebanon and Syria. In 1922, the British divided Palestine into two parts in order to create the country of Transjordan. Technically, then, all Israelis and Jordanians are also Palestinians and it therefore makes relatively little sense to speak of a dispute between Israelis and Palestinians. That use of the term is obsolete, and the people who now commonly refer to themselves as Palestinians and seek a new, independent state usually identify Palestine as an area that includes the West Bank, Gaza, and perhaps a portion of Jerusalem. The problem is that there is no universal agreement about what land is defined as Palestine, and the disagreements about this lead to confusion, misunderstanding, and conflict.

IDENTITIES

In order to speak sensibly about the Middle East, one must be able to refer to the various people who live there, but this is not as simple as it seems. The terms that are commonly used often suggest a single, simple image to those in the West, but when one looks more closely at the people of the Middle East, one begins to appreciate the tremendous variety comprised by the people under every convenient label used to define them. There are hundreds of different groups in the Middle East; the following three are chosen because they are, in a way, the most basic for an understanding of the region. These remarks are not designed so much to define these identities as to indicate the problems with attempting to define them.

What is an Arab?

The term "Arab" has no accepted derivation, although it seems to have been used at one time to distinguish nomads from city dwellers. The term has also been used to identify those from the Arabian peninsula, whether they are nomads or city dwellers, who participate in the way of life common to the region. Although one could take an etymological approach to this question and trace the use of the term in history and literature, this would not necessarily be helpful to understanding the contemporary use of the word. An Arab is more than someone who simply speaks Arabic, but he or she does not possess a single, identifiable trait based on beliefs, dress, diet, or action. Arabs are not a race. Arabs live both in the city and in the country and are influenced by the social traditions of their various locales. Many Arabs are Muslim, but some are not, and most Muslims are not Arabs. According to the American Arab Anti-Discrimination Committee, only one of the five largest Muslim countries (Egypt) is an Arabic country:

Indonesia	144 million Muslims
Pakistan	92 million Muslims
Bangladesh	90 million Muslims
India	90 million Muslims
Turkey	50 million Muslims
Egypt	44 million Muslims
Iran	44 million Muslims
Nigeria	40 million Muslims
United States	6 million (estimated)

There are millions of Christian Arabs. Approximately 8–12 percent of the Arab population around the world is Christian, and there are Jewish Arabs as well.[2]

Many have a single image of Arab women, but there is in fact great diversity here as well. Some Arab women are very traditional; they wear traditional clothing and play traditional roles within the home. However, many Arab women do not wear traditional clothing, are highly educated, and serve in their countries' legislatures as leaders of their people. There are Arab women who work as doctors, lawyers, and educators.

Some scholars have suggested that Arabic identity has to be understood as socially constructed; in other words, rather than having a distinct meaning, the term reflects an evolving sense of identity, sometimes generated by the people themselves and sometimes imposed upon them from without.

What is a Jew?

Tremendous variety is also found among Jews. There are, first of all, three major divisions of the religion, based on different understandings of revelation: Orthodox, Conservative, and Reform. The Orthodox believe that the *Tanach* [Hebrew Scriptures, including *Torah* ("teaching"), *Neviim* ("Prophets"), and *Ketuvim* ("writings")] is divinely revealed, but the Conservative and Reform Jews believe that the Tanach is a human document, although inspired by God. The Orthodox also believe that the Talmud (study, a book of laws, religious debate, ethical inquiry, and stories) is divinely revealed, while the Conservative and Reform see the Talmud as a very important book in their tradition, but not a book that is binding on them in any way. The view of revelation has obvious consequences for practice. While the Tanach and the Talmud provide a center of focus for all Jews, the Orthodox tend to be more traditional in their practice, although there are exceptions, and the Conservative and Reform tend to be more liberal in their practice, although there are again exceptions.

Crossing the boundaries of these three branches of Judaism are ethnic and racial distinctions that are also important. The two largest ethnic groups are Jews of Spanish descent (Sephardim) and Jews of German and Eastern European descent (Ashkenazim). These groups add their own flavor to Judaism, with different social traditions, different melodies to traditional songs, different pronunciation of Hebrew, and different foods. There are other important ethnic and racial distinctions because Jews live in almost every part of the world. There are Jews from China and Japan that do not look like Jews from Spain or Germany, and until recently, there was a large community of Black Jews in Ethiopia, many of whom now live in Israel. While all these different people share a religion, they don't always understand one another or cooperate with one another. There are the normal tensions, misunderstandings, and animosities among Jews that one would expect in any religion. In the state of Israel, there is a heated controversy about the legal definition of a Jew. Since the Orthodox are recognized by law as the group empowered to (among other things) perform Jewish marriage ceremonies, certify divorces, and recognize conversions, this controversy is both serious and emotional. At this point, for example, the Orthodox community in Israel would not accept as Jewish someone who was converted in the United States by a Reform rabbi. In addition to this, the Orthodox movement does not accept women as rabbis, whereas the Conservative and Reform movements do. In recent years, Conservative and Reform Jews have fought to have their branches of Judaism accepted under Israeli law on an equal basis with the Orthodox.

In spite of these differences, all Jews share a belief in one God, which is articulated in their most fundamental prayer (or declaration of faith), the Shema: "Hear, O Israel, the Lord is our God, the Lord is One. Blessed is His glorious kingdom for ever and ever." Traditionally, this prayer is recited three times a day. Jews everywhere believe that God requires that they strive to lead lives devoted to goodness as defined by their fundamental texts. The Ten Commandments announce what are widely known as the foundational beliefs of the Jews, but according to tradition, there are actually 613 commandments (*mitzvot,* which really means "good deeds"). What are these good deeds? They are defined with remarkable simplicity by Hillel, a Jewish teacher and contemporary of Jesus, who was once asked to explain the whole Torah. He said: "What is hateful to you, do not do to others. The rest is commentary; go and study." Additional guidance comes from the part of the Talmud known as the *Ethics of the Fathers:* "The world is sustained by three things: by the Torah, by worship, and by loving deeds." The quest for a good life guided by these principles represents a lifelong goal for Jews everywhere.

This statement about the religion is not sufficient, because there are observant Jews and nonobservant Jews. Some Jews follow the dietary restrictions of the

Torah or Talmud and do not eat pork, but some Jews eat pork and see no problem with the practice. Some identify with the religion even though they have lost their faith in God. Is an Arabic-speaking Jewish atheist in Yemen still a Jew? Is he or she an Arab? No clear answer presents itself.

What is a Muslim?

There are many different kinds of Muslims. The most visible division, however, is between the Sunni and the Shii. When Muhammad died in the year 632 C.E., a dispute arose about who his proper successor should be. Many supported Abu Bakr, who was Muhammad's father-in-law and close adviser. The system of caliphs ("deputies" or "successors") was soon established under him, with leaders chosen by a committee and sworn to allegiance. Others believed that leadership should remain within Muhammad's family and supported his cousin and son-in-law, Ali. Although Ali was finally chosen as the fourth caliph, he was murdered and his rule was not passed on to his son. The central difference between the Sunni ("those who accept customary practice") and the Shii ("the party [of Ali]") had to do with the religious status of the leader. The caliph was responsible for protecting the religious community, but he was not seen as someone with special religious authority. The Shii believe that only a direct descendant of Muhammad should serve as the leader (Imam) of the community; his link with the Prophet gives him special inspiration and insight into the religion. Over the years, additional differences developed between these two groups as they responded to the developments of history. Today, approximately 90 percent of Muslims are Sunni, but the Shii continue to make an important contribution to the religion and to the world.

With over a billion Muslims in the world, it should be obvious that there is a great variety among them in appearance, habits, dress, language, and practice. Some Muslims in the Middle East follow traditions handed down by French colonialists, wear Western dress, and speak French. Others follow Arabic traditions, wear the traditional dress of their region, and speak Arabic. There are caucasian Muslims, Chinese Muslims, and African-American Muslims; their acceptance of God as the center of their lives is what identifies them, not the color of their skin. There are approximately 140 million Muslims in Indonesia and over 270 million in the Indian subcontinent. The southern provinces of the former Soviet Union contain more than 50 million Muslims. In other words, more Muslims live outside the Middle East than inside the Middle East. One practice commonly associated with Islam is the tradition of veiling for women. However, the Quran does not actually require that women wear a veil in public. The Quran demands modesty, but not a particular kind of dress. The veil itself comes from Persian and Byzantine traditions, even though it is often assumed in the West that the Islamic view of women is defined by the veil. Women in Muslim countries have not always been given the opportunities actually offered to them by the Quran. Religion and social tradition have not always grown together.

Muslims share a belief in one God (Allah) with Jews and Christians. Islam literally means submission to God, and the word "Muslim" comes from the same root, meaning one who submits to God. The fundamental text for Muslims is, of course, the Quran ("recital"). It is understood to be a divinely inspired text that draws on the earlier revelations of the Hebrew Scriptures and the New Testament, both of which are honored by Muslims, although these earlier texts are seen as having been corrupted by time and therefore not entirely reliable. Many Muslims spend years committing the entire Quran to memory. The second most important source for religious truth in Islam is known as the Hadith ("traditions"), which is divided into two parts: the matri ("text") and the isnad ("chain of transmitters"). In other words, a Muslim can turn to the Hadith to discover the authoritative traditions of his or her religion as passed down by the Prophet to specific people, who then in turn passed reports down to others.

Islam offers a comprehensive guide for learning how to lead a life of goodness and stands on what are known as the Five Pillars. In that respect, it has a great deal in common with Judaism and Christianity. First of all, a Muslim must proclaim his or her faith in the unity of God and the importance of Muhammad: "There is no god but the God (Allah) and Muhammad is the messenger of God." Note that the word Allah is simply the Arabic word for God; it does not suggest anything different from the English word God. Also, it is important to recognize that Muhammad is not seen as the founder of Islam, which has always existed; rather, Muhammad is the final prophet. Secondly, a Muslim must pray five times a day to praise God, ask for guidance, and to offer greetings of peace. Observant Muslims therefore make prayer a constant presence in their lives. The Third Pillar is the requirement of almsgiving, or the obligation to take care of those in need. Muslims who are capable of giving are required either individually or through their governments to offer a certain amount of their wealth to the poor. The Fourth Pillar is the obligation to fast on Ramadan, which is a month during which all the devout (health permitting) fast from sunrise to sunset. This is a month for serious reflection about one's life and includes a number of celebrations, including ceremonial readings of the Quran. The final Pillar is the exhortation to pilgrimmage (Hajj). While it is always a blessing to visit Mecca, all adult Muslims who are able to do so must attempt a pilgrimmage at least once in their lives. The culmination of the pilgrimmage is an encounter with the Kaba, a house which Muslims believe was originally built by Abraham and the son he had by his wife's servant, Ishmael. The Kaba contains a black stone Muslims believe was given to Abraham by the angel Gabriel. A pilgrimmage to Mecca can be a life-changing experience for a Muslim.

There are still problems beneath the surface. As it is with Jews, so too it is with Muslims. There are observant and nonobservant Muslims. Some Muslims will eat pork and some will not. Some Muslims pray five times a day, and some no longer believe that God exists. Should one deny the identity of an atheistic Muslim who still believes that he or she is a Muslim? No easy set of definitions presents itself to settle these questions.

This introduction has attempted to make a simple but important point: the Middle East is characterized by complexity and diversity. The language, geography, and identities of the people cannot be defined easily. This is why the archeologist's approach is probably the best. One must strip away one layer of understanding after another, in search of the truth. At the same time, one must question one's assumptions and always be open to new possibilities.

This book is organized somewhat differently from other books on the Middle East, in that it begins by examining American perceptions of the region. Most Americans identify the Middle East with oil, so this book begins by looking at its importance. The Gulf War is another major topic that connects Americans with the Middle East. The book then moves to a treatment of the unfortunate stereotypes in the news and entertainment media that color American perceptions of the Middle East. Once American perceptions are analyzed, the book moves to a deeper level of analysis by examining the way in which history influences today's politics in the Middle East. Finally, the book turns to the ways in which the world is changing. Chapters on modernization, the war on terrorism, and the peace process offer some insights into chances for peace in the future.

Selected Bibliography

Esposito, John, *Islam: The Straight Path* (Oxford: Oxford University Press, 1991).

Khalidi, Rashid, *Palestinian Identity* (New York: Columbia University Press, 1997).

Endnotes

1. Sami Zubaida, *Islam: The People and the State* (I.B. Tauris and Co., Ltd: London, 1993) pp. 2–3. He says that "throughout the Islamic centuries after Muhammad and his immediate successors, religion and the state were united only in theory: in practice, as we shall see, there was a clear differentiation, a state of affairs accepted and rationalized by the ulama. In most of the modern states in Islamic countries, this de facto differentiation has become de jure, in that the application of *shaira* law is explicitly confined to areas of personal and family affairs, while all affairs of state and society are regulated by secular codes."

2. "Arab Stereotypes/Arab Reality," Arab Anti-Discrimination Committee, www.adc.org.

Chapter 1

The Politics of Oil

T he character of the Middle East is reflected in the complexity and diversity of its economic problems. The prospects for peace in the Middle East may in many important respects depend on the satisfactory handling of a number of basic economic issues, and oil continues to dominate the economies of many of the countries in the region. The actual challenges to oil-producing countries of the Middle East are significant, but they are not well understood in the West, at least within the general population. Most Americans see the oil-producing countries of the Middle East as economically powerful and dangerous. Their perceptions of the Middle East are often based on the impact of oil and gasoline prices in the United States. This chapter will focus on the disparity between American perceptions of the role of oil in the Middle East and the reality of that role.

In the summer of 2000, rising gasoline prices in the United States became a political issue. Truckers staged a protest by driving in a caravan through Washington, D.C. Vacationers complained that they would have to shorten their trips. Lower-income citizens worried about paying their heating bills the following winter. Gas prices became an issue in the presidential campaign at the time, and both Al Gore and George W. Bush were forced to make public statements about the problem. Who was responsible? Was it the rich oil companies, the environmental policies of the Clinton administration, or was it OPEC (Organization of Petroleum Exporting Countries)? Americans use a great deal of oil and feel very vulnerable when the supply seems threatened. This sense of vulnerability was especially noticeable in 1973, when oil-producing countries led by King Feisal of Saudi Arabia imposed an oil embargo on the United States for supporting Israel in the Arab-Israeli war that year. For the first time since World War II, people experienced gas rationing. In many cities, gas could only be purchased on certain days and under certain conditions, and gas stations often closed in the middle of business days after running out of gas. People in the United States were angry; they resented having smaller, less powerful countries in the Middle East exert such an influence on their lives. It seemed natural for Americans to entertain even the most radical ideas for how to solve the problem of dependency on foreign oil. Even war did not seem unreasonable to many.

Since 1973, many Americans have continued to see things from this perspective. Having inexpensive gas for their cars and for heating is almost seen as a right, and any time gas prices rise, the oil-producing countries of the Middle East are seen as responsible, regardless of the problems being faced by the oil-producing countries and regardless of completely independent economic factors that often affect oil prices. Most Americans do not want to hear about problems with refinery outputs or domestic distribution problems in the United States, and most are completely unaware of the cutbacks in the 1990s by American oil companies in exploration or development of new oil resources.[1] Most people want easy answers and someone to blame, and it is easier to blame the oil-producing countries of the Middle East.

Oil was not important to the world as recently as 1859, when it was first drilled in Pennsylvania.[2] Henry Ford's development of assembly-line production of automobiles in 1903 was largely responsible for changing the world. In 1914, Ford sold 10,000 Model T's, and the next year production increased to 250,000. In 1920, the total production of cars in the United States was 9.2 million. By 1927, the Ford Motor Company alone had sold over 15 million Model T's. This also changed the face of warfare. Trucks were used to move troops, tanks were developed for battle, and new ships were constructed to use oil rather than coal for fuel. By the end of World War I, the countries engaged in conflict had built over 200,000 planes to aid the war effort.

As oil became more important, oil companies became more powerful, and a battle began in American politics to address this issue. Standard Oil was dismantled after it was judged to be a monopoly, and a number of new companies came on the scene. In England, Winston Churchill supported the conversion of the British navy from coal to oil, even though it was clear that Britain would have to find outside sources of oil in order to do so. By the end of World War I, the demand for oil throughout the world had increased dramatically, and in the United States, which had until this time been a comfortable oil producer, this demand for the first time exceeded supply. Today, the United States consumes about 25 percent of the world's average daily output of oil and imports approximately half its oil. By 1999, the United States was importing 15 percent of its oil from Saudi Arabia, which replaced Venezuela as the nation's chief supplier.[3] The Middle East is more important than ever to American prosperity and security. Oil has not been a simple benefit to the producing nations of the Middle East, as the following sketches of Iran and Iraq will show.

IRAN

The oil industry of the Middle East began in Iran, and its development was initially controlled by Great Britain. The motive for turning to Iran was self-interest, and Britain assumed that as a world leader it had the right to control the conditions in Iran that would make it possible to obtain oil. In 1912, Winston Churchill decided that the British government should take over a British oil company that had discovered oil in Iran, but which was in poor financial condition. The government would buy 51 percent of the company's shares and would receive oil at a reduced rate for 20 years. The Persian government was not consulted, even though it had only given permission for a private oil company to operate within its borders. As Farmanfarmaian has pointed out:

To Persia this was a crushing blow. The Admiralty agreement alone meant it would suffer huge losses in profits. But Britain was the early twentieth century's superpower . . . To cry foul to a partner that was the British government was very different from accusing a private individual of concessionary violations. The Persian government no longer enjoyed the luxury of terminating the arrangement as a business deal; to threaten cancellation would now be to risk a losing war.[4]

The British arrangement went through many different forms as agreements were modified. In 1933, for example, Reza Shah negotiated a new version of the British deal that was to extend to 1993. The agreement guaranteed Iran a percentage of royalties that was not dependent upon the price of oil, and required an increase in the employment of Iranians in the industry, but was seen as a whole as unfavorable to Iran. Everything changed with the coming of the second World War. Reza Shah was suspected of pro-German sympathies and was forced by the Allies to abdicate in 1941, leaving his son, Muhammad Reza Shah, who was 22 when he assumed the throne, the harsh task of ruling in a country where he had no real power. The country descended into turmoil as tribal and religious leaders attempted to regain the power they had enjoyed before Reza Shah, and Marxists increased their power. All domestic problems were shaped under the shadow of foreign influence.

Politics and oil were combined in the political struggles that followed. A new leader emerged, Muhammad Mossaddiq, who challenged the young Shah for his repressive approach to rule and for accepting and promoting foreign influence in the country through the oil companies. Mossaddiq became prime minister and supported the nationalization of the Iranian oil industry, a move that prompted a number of countries, including Britain and the United States, to boycott Iranian oil. Mossaddiq refused to reverse his oil policy, even though the country was crippled economically by the boycott. In fact, he moved to broaden and strengthen the democratic institutions of the country. Mossaddiq never had the support of the army, the religious authorities (the ulama) did not endorse the secular character of his policies, and he was vulnerable. In its quest for oil security, the United States decided to use its power to intervene directly in Iranian politics and return a dictator to power. The American government was determined to prevent the Soviet Union from gaining influence in Iran, and it was not especially concerned with the effects our policies might have on the government or the people of Iran.

Muhammad Reza Shah renewed his relationship with Britain and America, the boycott was lifted, and Iran found itself once again with a repressive government under the influence of foreign powers. But economic conditions improved, and the Shah used profits from the remarkable rise in oil prices at the time to solidify his rule. He began to explore the full potential of what became a legendary secret security force (SAVAK, the intelligence and security organization, formed in 1957) to track down and neutralize political opponents; he lavished privileges on the army, and he attempted to buy acceptance from the people. This was the essence of what was known as the White Revolution.

The Shah's program of reform was, in some ways, beneficial. Roads were built, communications were improved, and health care and education received serious attention for the first time. These changes, however, were in many ways designed to mask the political repression behind them. In the mid–1960s, the Shah arrested and expelled a popular religious critic by the name of Ayatollah Ruhollah Khomeini, and in the mid–1970s, he eliminated all opposition political parties. While he was oppressing his own people, he was accepting hundreds of millions of dollars in military equipment and aid from Britain and the United States. Funds from increasing oil prices also made a significant contribution to the Shah's power. Within one year of the Arab oil embargo Iran's profits increased from $2.4 billion to $17 billion, and he used this money thoughtfully.[5] However, this harsh combination of economic boom and tyranny was not sufficient to sustain him. In 1979, Khomeini returned to lead a religious revival based in many ways on resentments stemming from the role that oil had played in Iranian history. The Shah was driven from power, and the United States became the "great Satan."

Khomeini did not focus his attention on economic matters, and the country suffered as a result. Some initial efforts were made to redistribute land and to address other economic issues, but the power struggles within Iran and the war with Iraq overpowered any attempts at economic reform. Falling oil prices created serious problems for the country. Unemployment rose, rationing was imposed, inflation increased, and budget deficits grew. In spite of this, the Iranian government provided subsidies for wheat and other basic commodities so that low prices would be artificially maintained.[6] Khomeini worked to establish his interpretation of Islamic law (*sharia*) as the foundation for the country's laws. This consumed much of the government's energy and attention. The modesty of women was enforced, adultery and homosexuality were condemned as capital offenses, and secular judges were dismissed from the courts. After Khomeini's death in 1989, politics was informed by a more practical perspective, even though Islam was still the foundation of the regime's legitimacy. Oil was still the main source of money for the government, even though income when adjusted for inflation was below that of the 1970s. Iran's successive governments have faced continued economic challenges related to their dependence on oil.

Today, the main weakness of the Iranian economy remains its overdependence on oil as a source of revenue. This, combined with high rates of unemployment, inflation, and serious income disparities, continues to create problems for the country. When oil prices declined in 1998, revenue from oil decreased 40 percent and trade deficits were recorded for the first time since 1993. When oil prices recovered, the Iranian economy began to recover quickly. Iran is attempting to deal with the problem of oil dependency. President Sayed Muhammad Khatami, who assumed office in 1997, has promoted the development of a stabilization fund to be used primarily in the event that international oil prices decline again. The government also announced its Third Five-Year Development Plan in March of 2000, which has as its primary goal the reduction of the economy's dependence on oil. The plan also allows for the private ownership of banks for the first time in Iran. Dependence on oil continues to create problems for the Iranian economy, but attempts are being made to address the issue.[7]

IRAQ

Initially, the oil industry in Iraq was controlled by international capital, especially from Britain and the United States. Shortly after World War I, Britain established Amir Feisal Ibn Hussein as king and sought to encourage some level of Iraqi independence, if only to secure Feisal's position and British interests. Oil was especially important, and the British imposed a treaty on Iraq in 1925 that allowed for a 75-year deal in which Britain would own the Iraq Petroleum Company (IPC) and give only a small fraction of the profit to Iraq. In 1932, Iraq became independent in a formal sense when the British mandate ended, but Britain was determined to maintain its control over the country and its oil. In a 1932 treaty, Britain was given the right to keep all its air bases operational, and Iraq agreed to consult with Britain on all foreign policy issues relevant to British interests. This treaty was supported by the wealthy classes in Iraq that Britain found it convenient to support, but opposition parties in Iraq criticized the treaty as another example of British imperialism.

Between 1930 and 1950, the IPC spent over $90 million in Western capital markets to support this industry and only $6 million in Iraq. Although there were some initial benefits to Iraq when roads, housing, and pipelines were built, the domestic labor force was not significantly influenced by the oil industry. Only 2.7 percent of the nonagricultural labor force in Iraq was used by the industry between 1929 and 1953.[8]

The small Iraqi labor force was not treated well, and workers began to organize. In June of 1946, after a request for a pay increase was rejected, 5,000 workers went on strike. The IPC demanded government support, and riot police raided a meeting of the workers, killing 6 and wounding 14. After this, tension grew between workers and what they perceived to be the British interests that supported the country's establishment.

Shortly after World War II, American oil companies became more active in the Middle East, establishing relationships with Saudi Arabia and Kuwait, and growing resentment toward Britain produced changes in Iraq. Inspired by the nationalization of the oil industry in Iran under the Mossaddiq regime, a resolution was introduced in the Iraqi parliament to follow the Iranian example. A new agreement with Britain was concluded in 1952 that provided for a 50–50 profit share, finally giving Iraq the opportunity to profit from its oil reserves. The increase in capital was not sufficient to radically improve conditions in Iraq, especially since the decisions on how to allocate funds were decisively influenced by powers serving their own self-interest. In other words, oil revenues did help the Iraqi economy in some ways, but they were not sufficient to encourage real economic development.[9] The Iraqi Development Board reflected the interests and perspectives of the wealthy class and sponsored projects that helped them increase their wealth and secure their position in the country. In fact, the increase in oil revenues allowed the existing Iraqi government to isolate itself from the needs of the majority of its own people, much in the same way that the Shah's regime distanced itself from all but the wealthy elite in Iran. By the late 1950s, a significant majority of the people still lived in poverty.

The government continued to pursue policies that perpetuated foreign influence in the country. In 1955, the Iraqi government signed the Baghdad Pact, an American-sponsored agreement of military cooperation with Britain and Turkey (and later Iran and Pakistan) designed to frustrate Soviet expansionist designs in the region. While oil revenues were increasing as a result of new arrangements and while political autonomy was increasing, Iraq remained dominated by outside powers.

In many ways, oil money may have created the conditions that led to the 1958 revolt and overthrow of the existing government. A bloody coup ended the monarchy that had been established by Britain and supported by them since World War I. King Feisal II and Nuri al Said, the prime minister, were murdered. The new military ruler withdrew from the Baghdad Pact and turned to the Soviet Union for support. A series of military governments held power between 1958 and 1968, when the Baath Party gained political prominence and provided a mechanism for the ambitions of Saddam Hussein, who rose steadily in party ranks until he became president in 1979. Throughout this period, oil remained central to the country's fate.

The IPC, until the time of Saddam Hussein, was still under foreign control, with Britain the dominant partner. In 1972, the Baath Party finally nationalized the oil industry, just in time to benefit from the huge increases in oil prices in 1973. Oil profits increased from approximately $900 million in 1971 to $9 billion in 1976 and then on to more than $21 billion in 1979. Nationalization of the industry helped legitimize the Baath Party, which then used the new wealth brought by oil sales to consolidate its power. Money from oil revenues was used to provide food subsidies and health care, and to reduce taxes.

Hussein accomplished much for his people. He attempted to take power away from wealthy landlords, he put people to work, and he attempted to improve the status of women. These new benefits often deflected attention from his use of oil profits to develop what has been referred to as the "technologies of coercion."[10] He developed a ruthless secret police to destroy political enemies, and he worked to develop weapons of mass destruction to enhance his influence in international affairs. Violence against the people became a standard feature of the government. By the time war broke out with Iran in 1980, Iraq was already in economic trouble and was borrowing significantly from other countries, including Kuwait and Saudi Arabia. The eight-year war was devastating for the weak economy; its total cost was over $400 billion.

Economic factors were not the only causes of the Gulf War, but they were important to Hussein's decision to invade Kuwait in 1991. He argued that oil prices were low because some countries like Kuwait were overproducing. If Iraq had been able to take over control of the oil reserves in Kuwait, it would have dominated 20 percent of the world's oil. But Hussein miscalculated and was opposed successfully by a multinational force. Hussein has managed to survive several coup attempts since the end of the war and to stay in power.

According to a United Nations report, the Gulf War "wrought near apocalyptic results on the economic infrastructure." Before sanctions were imposed by the United Nations, oil accounted for over 50 percent of the country's total revenue. The economic sanctions imposed by the United Nations and the limited sales of oil they permitted to pay for humanitarian aid in the years following have left the Iraqi economy weak. If the impediments to the economy related to war are overcome, Iraq will still have to face problems related to an underdeveloped industrial base and poor agriculture.[11]

THE NEGATIVE IMPACT OF OIL IN THE MIDDLE EAST

Few Americans are aware of the negative impact that oil has had in the Middle East, preferring instead to see the oil-producing countries there as rich and vaguely sinister, capable of controlling the United States at any moment by decreasing oil production or raising oil prices. Until 1960, when OPEC was founded, countries in the Middle East had very little control over oil production. The various European and American companies involved in the production of oil had, by then, arranged contracts that gave countries like Iran and Iraq a stronger share of profits than they had in the 1930s and 1940s. However, foreign interests still controlled refining, marketing, and production, which meant that prices were set by these interests as well. What the oil-producing countries wanted was a chance to break free from outside control; this was the primary motivating factor in the creation of OPEC. Until 1960, then, American companies still had a decisive say in how much oil would be produced and how much it would cost Americans to buy it. This assured strong economic growth in the United States and elsewhere, while denying the oil-producing states themselves the opportunity to develop. Gradually, OPEC began to work to raise oil prices to what it considered to be a fair level. It was not until 1973 that oil was used as a political weapon. The oil embargo supported an Arab political agenda, but it also brought oil prices up to a level that allowed the first opportunity for real economic growth in the OPEC nations. In spite of this opportunity, there are three main ways in which success in the oil industry has hurt the very nations that produce it: (1) it has led countries to ignore or slight other important elements of the economy; (2) it has unleashed forces that have challenged social traditions; (3) it has provided opportunities for traditional and repressive governments to ignore or minimize their responses to calls for political liberalization among their own people.

OPEC: The Organization of the Petroleum Exporting Countries

This organization was established in 1960 to link countries whose main source of economic strength is petroleum. It attempts to unify and coordinate the petroleum policies of members and to safeguard their interests. OPEC's share of world petroleum production was 40.8 percent in 1999 (compared with 54.7 percent in 1974). Member nations hold approximately 75 percent of the world's known reserves of crude petroleum; two-thirds of these reserves are in the Middle East. OPEC nations also possess approximately 43.2 percent of known reserves of natural gas. The members of OPEC are Algeria, Indonesia, Iran, Iraq, Kuwait, Libya, Nigeria, Qatar, Saudi Arabia, United Arab Emirates, and Venezuela. The web site for OPEC is www.opec.org.

Source: *The Europa World Yearbook: 2001*

ECONOMIC STAGNATION

Most of the oil-producing countries have failed to devote sufficient attention to the development of the broader economy. The incredible boom in the mid-1970s served as a temptation to, in a sense, avoid reality. This is particularly noticeable in the area of agriculture. All the countries in the region have difficulty producing enough food for their people; in fact, agricultural imports are higher in the Middle East than anywhere else in the world.[12] During the 1970s and 1980s, it seemed to make more sense for oil-producing nations to import food, which they could well afford, than to concentrate on making long-term changes in the agricultural industry. During this time, food imports reached $25 billion annually, which is approximately 10 times what they had been before the oil boom. Some countries had limited success promoting agriculture. Saudi Arabia has significantly increased the amount of land under cultivation, but it remains one of the largest food importers in the world.

Manufacturing is another neglected part of the economies in oil-producing states. The first problem is one of natural resources. In order to produce manufactured goods, they would have to import metals like iron, steel, and aluminum. Importing metal is not the only problem. Machine tools, furnaces, and other manufacturing equipment would also need to be imported in order to create the needed factories.[13] A good example of this problem is the Riyadh Wooden Door Company of Saudi Arabia. It was formed in the late 1980s and is often cited as an example of the growing strength of Saudi industry. But, as an important study of the Saudi economy has pointed out:

> In addition to the workers, all materials were imported, including the wood, glue, and, of course, machinery. Profitability was also dependent on subsidized electricity, subsidized water, and subsidized finance. Riyadh Wooden Door Company thus amply illustrates the short-comings of the Kingdom's non-oil industrial enterprises, specifically their dependence on subsidies, foreign workers, and imported materials.[14]

There is yet another problem. The domestic market for manufactured goods has yet to be developed and may have inherent limitations. A country such as Saudi Arabia would have to import many raw materials, import machinery to build factories, and then export many of the products it produces. This is an expensive process and one that doesn't seem to make much sense as long as oil money is pouring into the country. There have been improvements in Middle Eastern manufacturing, but they have not been significant enough to transform the economies of these states in a fundamental way.

An odd dynamic has been developing in the region. Increased oil revenues encouraged oil-producing nations to import food, partly to placate their populations. More food and better food, along with better health care, has increased population growth. This, in turn, has created a greater demand for food. Also, the kind of food that is eaten is changing. An increasing number of people have made meat a regular part of their diets, and packaged foods are more popular than they were before 1970. Birth rates are traditionally high in the region, but until recently, death rates kept the population modest. In recent years, for example, infant mortality has dropped by more than 50 percent in many countries. In Saudi Arabia, infant mortality has dropped by 75 percent. The one exception to this is Iraq, where the aftermath of the Gulf War has had a dramatic impact. A report by the International Committee of the Red Cross in February, 2000, stated that infant mortality rates had increased three times what they had been before the imposition of sanctions in 1990. Iraq claims that the sanctions themselves have produced this increase; the United States has accused Saddam Hussein of diverting important food and medicine from the general population, causing the increase. Iraq is a special case; the infant mortality rates there are related in one way or another to the Gulf War and do not suggest any general economic trends in the region.

In addition to the general trend toward lower infant mortality, life expectancy has been extended from about 55 years to 64 or more. In the United States, it is widely understood that an increase in life expectancy has put a tremendous strain on the Social Security system. In the Middle East, it has created what is sometimes referred to as a "demographic revolution."[15] The population in the region as a whole is quite young. The average age in the Middle East is 16. These young people tend to be consumers of expensive products and services while being unable for the most part to generate much wealth. They are better fed and better educated than their parents, yet they have a difficult time finding work. Their youth makes their memories short. A 16-year old today would have never lived in a world before the oil boom and wouldn't remember or be impressed with the conditions under which people lived before that time. The economies of these countries have not been able to keep pace with the rise in population or with a rise in expectations that has accompanied the oil boom. Now that oil prices have declined and the oil boom has disappeared, countries are faced with high demands for food and services, but they have significantly lower resources available to them to meet those demands.

Debt continues to be a problem in the region, now that the oil boom is over. This has led to problems with credit. The Bank of England has called Saudi credit-worthiness into question, U.S. credit agencies have also expressed concern, and the International Monetary Fund has issued warnings. Populations have come to expect that their governments will provide what they have provided in the past. Once expectations are raised, it is difficult to frustrate them. Oil prices have begun to rise again in the last few years, and may perhaps allow for at least temporary relief from these problems. As recently as 1998, oil prices in the OPEC nations were, in the words of one scholar, in a "free fall," with crude oil prices at a 12-year low of below $10 a barrel.[16] Saudi Arabia was forced to make serious cutbacks in government expenditures in a number of areas, including social programs and public works. In addition, the government increased the price for services and pursued delinquent payments from consumers of public utilities. Prices began to rise again after that, partly as a result of the recovery of Asian economies, and have risen to over $30 a barrel. But increased oil prices do not represent a long-term solution. Saudi Arabia, for example, is looking into diversifying its economy and privatizing a number of state industries, including the Saudi Airlines, Saudi Consolidated Electric Companies, and Saudi Telecommunications.

SOCIAL TRANSFORMATION

The oil boom has contributed to fundamental social changes in the region, and not all of these changes are perceived as positive. New affluence has challenged the traditional family, which was at one time ordered around work and prayer. Traditional life in most of the Middle East was rural, poor, and hard. In 1902, less than 10 percent of the population in Saudi Arabia lived in cities. Shortly after World War II, major cities in Saudi Arabia were still quite small. Mecca's population was only about 40,000, and Riyadh held only 25,000.[17] The struggle to survive in this kind of world demanded constant effort, large families, and adherence to the moral code of the Koran. Travel was still difficult then, and entertainment that went beyond good conversation and simple music was rare. Oil money changed everything. Government subsidies improved health care and educational possibilities, but the work ethic was challenged. Housing became more plentiful as a result of government lending institutions, but this encouraged young married couples to establish homes separate from their parents and grandparents. Continuity between generations was interrupted. Other social changes followed, as these comments about Saudi Arabia show:

> The Kingdom's rulers and ulema may forbid the opening of movie theaters, but the Kingdom's video stores offer a wide variety of uncensored and definitely un-Wahhabi-like fare. Alcohol and tobacco may be condemned in the mosque, but private use abounds behind closed doors, and there is a thriving black market in Johnny Walker whiskey and the local home brew, *siddiqui,* or "friend." Photography may be shunned by some because it depicts the human image, but camera stores abound.[18]

Crime figures indicate that social changes are taking place. Within two years of the beginning of the oil boom, all crime in Saudi Arabia had increased. Drug and alcohol crimes, for example, increased 1,400 percent between 1971 and 1975. One reason for this is the tremendous disparity between the government's policies, which are still inspired by an interpretation of Islam, and the increasing number of young people used to the relative affluence introduced by the oil boom. The young are restless and crave entertainment, but the government of Saudi Arabia still prohibits most outlets for this energy. One important exception is soccer. The government has encouraged the game, but matches are often accompanied by improper behavior, and religious figures have been critical of the sport.

In many ways, the relative affluence introduced by oil money has created problems for traditional society, especially among the young. What is seen as moral corruption has led to new calls for religious purity. Economic changes have led to social changes, which in turn have in many ways encouraged some to hope for a religious return to the past.

POLITICAL STAGNATION

In many ways, oil money has allowed traditional power structures in the Middle East to survive challenges for reform. In Iran and Iraq, new wealth was not used to provide opportunities for political reform; rather, it was used to secure power through repression for the existing rulers. The Shah and Saddam Hussein built powerful internal security forces that were used to attack political enemies, including religious leaders. In Saudi Arabia, political reforms that were under discussion since the 1950s were abandoned when money offered opportunities to substitute benefits for increased participation. The reforms that had been discussed included the creation of a written constitution, the creation of a consultative council with real power, and substantial restrictions of the king's power. While these reforms were debated, the oil boom allowed the government to begin what became essentially a welfare state. Since the end of the Gulf War, Saudi Arabia has created a Consultative Council, but many have criticized it for being weak.

Oil money made it unnecessary for these governments to tax their people heavily. During the oil boom, for example, taxes were essentially nonexistent in Saudi Arabia. A well-respected book on Saudi Arabia states that "The combination of subsidies and government giveaways, plus the absence of taxes, led to massive enrichment of the Saudi people. As King Fahd bin Abdulaziz later noted, 'A Saudi has to be very unlucky, very stupid and very lazy not to do well.'"[19] It is a time-honored political principle that people are less inclined to protest a lack of freedom or a lack of participation than to protest a lack of benefits, and the boom years made it possible for governments to avoid turning to their own citizens for the funds needed to support the welfare state. But when recession hit, and governments were forced to cut back on subsidies or raise taxes, people were upset and political protests resulted.

Economic recession was largely responsible for encouraging Iran to turn away from the radical religious repression and international isolation that characterized the Khomeini regime. After Khomeini's death in 1989, there was some hope that true political pluralism might emerge in Iran, but nothing this fundamental has taken place. During most of Khomeini's rule, only one political party was allowed (until it was abolished by Khomeini), the Islamic Republican Party. President Hashemi Rafsanjani took over power after Khomeini's death and introduced a number of economic and social reforms, and Muhammad Khatami's election in 1997 signaled the beginning of a new era of tolerance. However, fundamental political reforms have yet to take place in Iran. In 1999, a law was passed that raised the voting age from 16 to 17, taking the right to vote away from 1.5 million young people.

While true reform has yet to take place, some attempts have been made to address international issues. In 1981, for example, the Gulf Cooperation Council (GCC) was founded by Saudi Arabia and five other traditional states in the Gulf region (Bahrain, Kuwait, Oman, Qatar, and United Arab Emirates). The GCC initially focused on defense issues raised by the Iran-Iraq War. In 1982, the ministers drew up a "unified economic agreement" that facilitated the abolition of custom duties, encouraged technical cooperation, and looked forward to harmonizing banking regulations. In 1985, the GCC developed a unified agricultural policy to work on water conservation, and to develop improvements in veterinary vaccines and fertilizers. Clearly, the GCC was not successful in protecting one of its member states, Kuwait, from being invaded in 1990, but the international organization at least brings these countries together for discussion; perhaps it will make a contribution to progress in the future.

It is a common American belief that the oil-producing countries of the Middle East are rich and arrogant, that they can exert a controlling influence on world affairs whenever it pleases them to do so. This chapter has argued that oil has been a mixed blessing in the Middle East. The profits of the oil boom years did make possible huge advances in transportation, communication, and health care, but a failure to expand the non-oil-producing elements of the economies led to a dependence on oil that proved disastrous when the oil boom ended in the early 1990s. In other words, the oil-producing countries of the Middle East are in some ways even more dependent upon oil than are their customers. For example, Saudi Arabia is the leading producer of oil in OPEC. It has reserves of approximately 260 billion barrels, which is one-fourth the world's total, and is capable of producing 8 million barrels a day. Its economy is decisively influenced by oil. Revenues from oil account for 35 percent of the gross national product, and 75 percent of government revenues are from oil. In addition, 90 percent of Saudi exports are related to oil. This is why oil prices are extremely important to Saudi Arabia. Dependence on oil has led to economic stagnation, disruptive social changes, and calls for political reform that have yet to be met. According to a report by the International Monetary Fund, oil price fluctuations continue to dominate economic developments in the Middle East. After falling by 20 percent in 1998, the terms of trade increased by 50 percent in 1999–2000 as oil prices recovered. Several increases in oil production by OPEC helped to preserve strong prices. Oil prices are expected to fall somewhat over the next few years, but most of the oil-producing nations have worked to use the windfall profits thoughtfully and the decreases should not be disastrous. Modest growth is therefore predicted, but Saudi Arabia, which still has significant government debt, needs to be especially prudent.[20] Most importantly, oil price instability emphasizes the need for oil-producing countries to push for reforms that will encourage economic diversification. The Gulf Cooperation Council countries need to expand the non-oil private sector in order to promote long-term economic growth. These economic realities will continue to have a significant impact on domestic and foreign policy in the region. Oil will influence the chances for peace, but not in the way that many Americans believe.

Selected Bibliography

Amuzegar, Jahangir, *Managing the Oil Wealth: OPEC's Windfalls and Pitfalls* (London: I.B. Tauris, 2001).

Farmanfarmaian, Manucher and Roxane, *Blood and Oil* (New York: Modern Library, 1999).

Obaid, Nawaf, *The Oil Kingdom at 100: Petroleum Policymaking in Saudi Arabia* (Washington, D.C.: The Washington Institute for Near East Policy, 2000).

Wilson, Peter, and Graham, Douglas, *Saudi Arabia: The Coming Storm* (Armonk, N.Y.: M.E. Sharpe, 1994).

Endnotes

1. See Brooks Wrampelmeier, review of *The Oil Kingdom at 100: Petroleum Policymaking in Saudi Arabia* in *Middle East Policy* (March, 2001: vol. 8, p. 163, 165.

2. This analysis of oil is indebted to the Manucher and Roxane Farmanfarmaian's fine treatment of the problem in *Blood and Oil* (Modern Library: New York, 1999).

3. Brooks Wrampelmeier, *Middle East Policy,* 165.

4. Manucher and Roxane Farmanfarmaian, *Blood and Oil* (New York: Modern Library, 1999), 90. This analysis of Iranian oil is indebted to Farmanfarmaian's book.

5. Sanda McKey, *The Iranians* (Penguin Books: New York, 1996), 256.

6. Sydney Fisher and William Ochsenwald, *The Middle East: A History* (New York: McGraw Hill, 1997), 527.

7. "Iran," *The Europa World Yearbook: 2001,* vol. 1, 42nd ed. (London: Europa Publications, 2001), 2,018.

8. Samira Haj, *The Making of Iraq 1900–1963: Capital, Power, and Ideology* (Albany: State University of New York Press, 1997), 70, 100, 138. This analysis of Iraq is indebted to Haj.

9. Haj, 72.

10. Haj, 138. See also Stephen Humphreys, *Between Memory and Desire* (Berkeley: University of California Press, 1999), 120. Humphreys traces the tradition of violence back to 1958.

11. See Barry Turner (ed.), *The Statesman's Yearbook: 2002* (New York: Palgrave Publishers, 2001), 906; and *The Europa World Yearbook: 2001.*

12. Peter Wilson and Douglas Graham, *Saudi Arabia: The Coming Storm* (Armonk, N.Y.: M.E. Sharpe, 1994), 217.

13. Humphries, 18.

14. Wilson and Graham, 217.

15. Humphreys, 6–7.

16. Moin A. Siddiqi, "Oil Update," *The Middle East,* September, 2000, 31.

17. Wilson and Graham, 234.

18. Wilson and Graham, 234, 238–239.

19. Wilson and Graham, 180.

20. *World Economic Outlook: May, 2001/Fiscal Policy and Macroeconomic Stability* (Washington, D.C.: International Monetary Fund, 2001).

Chapter 2

The Gulf War and Its Implications

When the Gulf War started, President Bush vowed that it would not become another Vietnam, and indeed the war was very different. Iraq was portrayed as an absolutely clear villain, and Saddam Hussein was compared to Hitler. The United States attacked with overwhelming force, instead of committing troops to fight a long-term, limited war. Bush set clear military objectives that could be met in a reasonable amount of time. He said that "If one American soldier has to go into battle, that soldier will have enough force behind him to win and then get out as soon as possible . . . I will never, ever agree to a halfway effort."[1] This was a war designed to produce a recognizable victory. The Vietnam War was characterized by morally ambiguous goals combined with a high number of casualties and no clear victory. When the Gulf War ended, the United States could claim victory, but Saddam Hussein was still in power and remained defiant. Today, Iraq is working to develop weapons of mass destruction and is still on the U.S. State Department's list of state sponsors of terrorism; many believe that Iraq continues to pose a serious threat to peace in the region. During the American attacks on the Taliban regime of Afghanistan following the September 11, 2001, attacks, President George W. Bush suggested that the United States might carry the War on Terrorism to other countries, and he implied that Iraq was one possible target. This chapter on the Gulf War is designed to offer some perspective and raise some questions about the continuing tensions in the region.

PRELUDE TO WAR

During the Iran-Iraq War (1980–1988), sometimes referred to as the first Gulf War, the United States supported Iraq. At that time, Iran was its perceived enemy; it was the home of what was becoming known as Islamic Fundamentalism, something that appeared to be an open challenge to the American regime in the same way that communism had been seen for so long. Saddam Hussein was a more recognizable figure for Americans. He was classified in the press as a "strongman" or a "military leader." His kind of rule was seen as flawed but familiar. As happened during the most difficult periods of the Cold War, the United States accepted Iraq as an unsavory ally, believing that it could be controlled. As the noted scholar John Esposito has pointed out:

> There are lessons to be learned from a past in which fear of a monolithic Soviet threat often blinded us to the humanity, values, and aspirations and diversity of the majority; led to uncritical support for regimes as long as they remained allies in the Cold War; enabled an easy acceptance of authoritarianism....[2]

The United States hoped to play the "Iraqi card" against Iran in much the same way that it once tried to play the "China card" against the Soviet Union. But the United States underestimated the problems that Saddam Hussein would later cause.

The Iran-Iraq war followed a long series of tensions between the two countries, especially over the rights to the Shatt al-Arab waterway as defined by the 1975 Algiers Agreement and the presence of Iranian forces in Abu Musa and the Tunb islands. Iraqi forces entered Iran in September of 1980, but Iranian forces were stronger than Iraq had anticipated and Iraq was driven back into its own territory by summer of that year. After a series of attacks and counterattacks, which included aerial attacks on oil fields and oil tankers in the Gulf, neither side had achieved a clear victory. In July of 1988, Iran announced that it had accepted a cease-fire negotiated by the United Nations during the previous year,

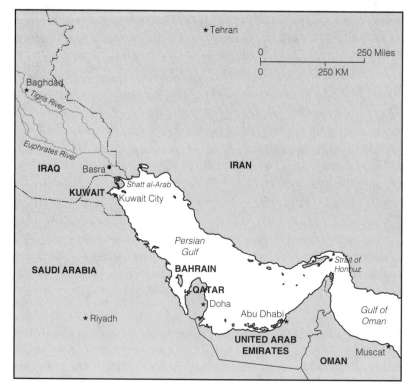

Figure 2 The Persian Gulf

and Iraq was willing to accept the terms of the Algiers Agreement. The war was devastating for both countries; each suffered massive casualties and neither had an economy capable of sustaining such a conflict.

Shortly after the cease-fire went into effect, Saddam Hussein began to move troops to the border of Kuwait. Iraq needed oil money in order to recover economically. At least $60 billion was owed to Kuwait, but Hussein argued that the debt should be forgiven since Iraq had essentially defended the entire region from Iran. In other words, Hussein argued that Iraqi debt existed because it had fought on behalf of its Arab neighbors; they should now show their appreciation by covering some of the costs. Also, Hussein complained that Kuwait had consistently exceeded the oil production quotas set by OPEC. He accused Kuwait of bringing oil prices down through overproduction and therefore making it more difficult for Iraq to recover its war losses. Some of this oil came from the Rumeila oil field, which Iraq had claimed as its own for many years.

Most Americans were unaware of the long-standing claim that Iraq made to Kuwait, a claim that had at least some foundation in history. As will be discussed in Chapter 4, none of the countries in the region has natural borders; all political boundaries were drawn up by imperial powers after World War I ended and the Ottoman Empire fell apart. Great Britain drew the Iraq-Kuwait border in 1923 and gave Kuwait more territory in the north than had traditionally been under the control of the Kuwaiti dynasty. This was an intentional act designed to limit Iraq's access to the Persian Gulf in order to prevent Iraq from establishing itself as an important naval power. Only Basra was left to provide access to the Gulf, and it was over 50 miles inland, up the Shatt al-Arab waterway. Iraq had not even recognized Kuwait as a country until 1963. On the other hand, the ruling Al-Sabah dynasty in Kuwait had a long history and a legitimate claim to the land.

In addition, the issue of access to the Gulf became more serious for Iraq after its conflict with Iran. Basra was badly damaged, leaving Iraq with no real port. Since pipelines were unreliable and costly, Iraq had no efficient, profitable way of distributing the oil it was able to produce.[3] From Iraq's standpoint, Kuwait was producing oil on land that really belonged to Iraq, turning its back on the nation that fought to protect it, denying reasonable accommodation to Iraqi requests for access to the Gulf, and artificially lowering oil prices. Iraq presented its attack on Kuwait as a defensive, not an offensive, action.

The United States has to bear some responsibility for Saddam Hussein's invasion of Kuwait. As recently as January of 1990, President George Bush had approved the sale of military equipment to Iraq. In the spring, the senatorial delegation headed by Senator Bob Dole (who was a candidate for the presidency in 1996) informed Saddam Hussein that the United States was interested in improving relations with Iraq. In an embarrassing moment for American diplomacy, the U.S. ambassador to Iraq, April Glaspie, did not challenge Saddam Hussein when he spoke of the possibility of using military force against Kuwait. She told him that the United States was essentially neutral on the subject of border disputes between Iraq and Kuwait. In Washington, the Assistant Secretary of State for Near East and South Asian Affairs testified before Congress that no current treaty obligations required that the United States respond if Kuwait were attacked. President Bush was praised after the Gulf War for standing up to Hussein and driving him out of Kuwait, but it is entirely possible that the Bush administration unintentionally sent signals to Hussein that Kuwait was not a high priority for the United States. At the very least it must be said that the United States did not make it clear to Hussein that he would be opposed if he should attack Kuwait.

THE MILITARY CAMPAIGN

Hussein began sending troops to the Kuwaiti border at the end of July, which worried Egyptian President Husni Mubarak enough to prompt him to fly to Baghdad. Hussein reassured Mubarak that he had no intention of sending troops into Kuwait unless all diplomatic avenues had been explored. Later, Mubarak expressed frustration with Hussein for misleading him. On August 2, the attack began, thinly disguised as a military action to protect Kuwait. A radio announcement stated:

> God helped the liberals from among the honest ranks to undermine the traitorous regime in Kuwait, who is involved in Zionist foreign schemes. The liberals from the sons of dear Kuwait appealed to the Iraqi leadership to provide support and backing to prevent any possibility [of takeover] by those who desire foreign interference in Kuwait's affairs and the end of its revolution. They have urged us to help restore security to spare the sons of Kuwait any harm.[4]

The invasion of Kuwait was accomplished easily. Saddam Hussein sent approximately 100,000 troops supported by 300 tanks across the border and surrounded the capital city in one night, easily overwhelming the Kuwaiti army of 16,000; the emir of Kuwait and his family fled into exile ahead of the advancing Iraqi forces. On August 8, Iraq announced that it had formally annexed Kuwait. Much to Hussein's surprise, opposition to his action was immediate. George Bush ordered an economic embargo on Iraq and froze all Iraqi and Kuwaiti assets in the United States. The United Nations followed almost immediately by passing Resolution 660, which condemned the invasion and demanded that Iraq withdraw its troops. The U.N. also declared the annexation of Kuwait to be illegal. In addition, the Arab League condemned Iraq's actions and demanded by a vote of 21 to 14 that Iraq withdraw from Kuwait immediately.

Once Iraq controlled Kuwait, it had power over 20 percent of the world's oil reserves, but Hussein's potential control of new oil was only part of what worried the West. Many were also concerned that he might extend his military campaign into Saudi Arabia, although there is no real evidence that this was ever one of his goals. In spite of their reluctance to invite American troops into their country, Saudi officials gave in to President Bush's admonitions. On August 2, President Bush ordered 200,000 troops into Saudi Arabia by October in what became known as Operation Desert Shield. America's first priority was not to drive Saddam Hussein out of Kuwait, but rather to keep him from advancing into Saudi Arabia.

President Bush worked to develop an international consensus opposing Hussein. A number of countries sent troops to Saudi Arabia to support Desert Shield, including Great Britain, Italy, and France. Bush also worked to involve Arab governments in the growing coalition. Egypt and Syria agreed to send troops to join the Desert Shield multinational force, but King Hussein of Jordan was critical of the U.S. response and decided to remain neutral, perhaps because a large proportion of Jordan's population identifies itself as Palestinian (this identification is related to the fact that Jordan itself was part of the territory originally identified as Palestine).

In November of 1990, the United Nations Security Council adopted Resolution 678, which authorized the use of all necessary means to enforce the withdrawal of Iraqi forces if they had not withdrawn by January 15, 1991. No progress was made toward a solution, and on January 16, 1991, the multinational force began air attacks on Iraq, led by General Colin Powell, chairman of the Joint Chiefs of Staff (later to become Secretary of State under George W. Bush). Operation Desert Shield became Operation Desert Storm.

Saddam Hussein had from the beginning attempted to link his invasion of Kuwait with the Arab-Israeli conflict, even though his reasons for the war had little to do with it. On August 12, he suggested that he might withdraw from Kuwait if Israel withdrew from the West Bank and Gaza. He undoubtedly understood that there was very little likelihood that Arabs and Israelis could fashion a settlement to their dispute in time to have any impact on the Kuwaiti occupation, but he hoped to broaden the focus of the conflict and direct attention away from Iraq's actions. The peace offer did have the advantage of presenting Saddam Hussein as a champion of the Palestinians, rather than a dictator interested in taking an Arab neighbor's oil by force. Hussein was sincere in at least one sense: He did believe that the United States was being hypocritical by confronting him for occupying Kuwait and ignoring U.N. Resolutions when it did not confront the Israelis for occupying the West Bank and Gaza and also ignoring U.N. resolutions. Saddam Hussein stridently asserted that Israel was the key to the problems in the region. The very first night of the bombing, the state-run radio issued a statement that "the mother of all battles" had begun:

> O great Iraqi people, sons of our great people, valiant men of our courageous armed forces . . . Satan's follower Bush committed his treacherous crime, he and the criminal Zionism. The great duel, the mother of all battles, between victorious right and the evil that will certainly be defeated has begun, God willing.[5]

Saddam sent SCUD missiles (Soviet-made short-range tactical missiles) into Israel, even though Israel had agreed to stay completely out of the conflict. Hussein may have hoped to lure the Israelis into responding to his attack, something that might well have undermined the coalition. It was amazing to see the unusual assortment of countries working together at all, but the support among Arab states was much stronger for Desert Shield than it was for Desert Storm. Israeli involvement would have broken the back of the delicate alliance. In order to encourage restraint on the part of the Israelis, President Bush sent what was known as the Patriot Missile Defense System to Israel to protect the Israelis from missile attacks. The Patriot system was praised at the time, but later studies found that it was no more than 10 percent effective. The SCUD attacks on Israel were partly successful and psychologically devastating to the Israeli population; Hussein threatened that he would use chemical weapons on his warheads, which invited people to compare Saddam Hussein with Hitler. The threats were taken seriously because he had not hesitated to use chemical weapons in the war with Iran and in military operations in his own country against dissident populations. Gas masks were issued to Israeli citizens as 12 missiles from Iraq landed in population centers in Haifa and Tel Aviv, but Hussein chose not to use the chemical weapons at his disposal, perhaps because he was concerned that such an action would increase support for Israel.

The coalition against Iraq gained control of the air very quickly. The bombing of Iraq was not intended to be cruel; targets were limited at least at first to military and intelligence facilities or to support facilities, but the fact is that many of the targets also served civilian needs. The general population suffered as a result of the air campaign. The United States went to great lengths to reassure its people that what were termed as "smart bombs" were being used in precision attacks. Videos of perfect bombings were shown over and over again on American television in order to support the military's contention that all was well. After the war, reports indicated that the smart bombs were not all that smart. Targets were missed and many civilians died as a result. In fact, a *Washington Post* report of a briefing by the Air Force Chief of Staff revealed that only 7 percent of the bombs dropped were precision-guided bombs. These were, indeed, 90 percent accurate, but the remaining bombs were unguided and were only 25 percent accurate.[6] The American public had been given the impression that its bombing was especially humane, while Saddam Hussein was sadistic, but the American air campaign did produce significant civilian suffering.

In February, the ground assault began, and lasted only 100 hours. It began after Iraqi forces had been significantly weakened and were completely without air support. The Iraqis that actually confronted American troops were poorly trained and poorly equipped conscripts from minority populations. They were also isolated, since important communication centers had been destroyed. The coalition attack drove back the Iraqi troops easily. Many surrendered and many were slaughtered from the air as they retreated on the road to Basra, which became known as the "highway of death." Questions were raised after the war about the ethical propriety of attacking a retreating army, but the Bush administration was determined to end the conflict as quickly as possible. A cease-fire was arranged on February 28, and Iraq renounced its annexation of Kuwait. U.N. Security Council Resolution 687 linked the removal of economic sanctions to Iraq's willingness to eliminate weapons of mass destruction from its arsenal. It also demanded that Iraq pay war reparations.

Before they fled Kuwait, Saddam Hussein's forces set hundreds of oil wells on fire and pumped oil into the Persian Gulf from a loading site south of Kuwait City. This oil slick eventually covered an area of approximately 240 square miles, making it one of the worst ecological disasters in history.[7] These attacks on the environment were designed to make it difficult for Kuwait to recover from the war. Kuwait would face real challenges as a result of the attacks on the environment because its economy and the welfare system supported by it is almost entirely dependent upon oil. The old pearling industry that had been the backbone of the economy in the early 1900s had long since disappeared. Saddam Hussein succeeded in harming Kuwait, even if he could not keep it.

Immediately after the cease-fire, two groups in Iraq responded to American encouragement and revolted against Saddam Hussein. The Shiite minority in southern and central Iraq and the Kurdish minority in northern Iraq both attempted to throw off the oppression of the Iraqi regime. However, the United States did little to support the people who had responded to our almost constant calls to the Iraqi people to revolt. Saddam Hussein quickly ended the Shiite revolt. Large-scale executions followed the end of the uprising. The Kurdish people were more organized, but the revolt was crushed ruthlessly. Over a million Kurds were forced to flee into the mountains and out of the country into Turkey and Iran. One result of this domestic conflict was that the U.N. established areas known as "safe havens" in the north, and the United States (along with France, Russia, and the United Kingdom) established a "no fly" zone in southern Iraq in order to assure the Shiite population they would face no further repercussions stemming from the revolt. This action was later endorsed by the United Nations.

THE DIPLOMATIC WAR

The stage was now set for a series of confrontations between Iraq and the U.N. and the United States. Saddam Hussein was determined to crush resistance, both in the form of revolutionary groups and in the more subtle form of competitors within the Baath Party. He was also determined to remain defiant in the face of the sanctions imposed by the U.N. He continued to launch attacks against the Shiite minority in the south, and in 1996 he once again sent forces into the north to attack one of the Kurdish factions. This action resulted in President Clinton's decision to order air strikes on military targets in southern Iraq to make Saddam Hussein "pay a price" for his actions.

Hussein also worked to secure his leadership by placing members of his family in important positions in the government. In spite of this, several attempted coups were reported, although they were unsuccessful and led to harsh reprisals. When two members of his family defected to Jordan and began to offer information to the West, Saddam Hussein lured them back to Iraq with promises of amnesty, but both were murdered shortly after they returned. In 1998, the U.N. Commission on Human Rights reported that at least 1,500 political opponents of Hussein had been executed, and several important Shiite leaders were also killed, although the Iraqi government denied that it had been involved.

Saddam Hussein refused to cooperate with the weapons inspectors assigned by the U.N. through its Special Commission (UNSCOM), as outlined in Resolution 715. The U.N. was reluctant to remove any of the economic sanctions that had been imposed on Iraq until full weapons inspection was allowed, and Saddam Hussein was determined to frustrate the work of the inspectors. UNSCOM was very aggressive in Iraq, and it managed to destroy more chemical and biological weapons after the war than had been destroyed by the coalition during the war. However, the inspectors became convinced that Saddam Hussein was allowing them access to some weapons while concealing others. Saddam Hussein worked to frustrate the inspectors and made periodic demands that they be removed from Iraq, claiming that they were agents of the CIA. This was strenuously denied by the United States, until it was discovered that some of the inspectors had, in fact, been supplying information to U.S. intelligence agencies. The U.N. was embarrassed and the inspection program was compromised.

Shortly after the war, world opinion began to turn against the United States, partly because the Iraqi people were clearly suffering as a result of the embargo, and partly because continued American bombing of Iraq was seen as unnecessary. Iraq worked to repair the damage done by the bombing it had endured, and in May of 1996, the U.N. worked out a compromise on oil sales. A growing uneasiness in the United States and with its Arab allies about the harsh effects of the embargo led the U.N. to allow Iraq to sell $1 billion in oil every three months, using the profits for humanitarian aid and war reparations. This policy could not be monitored closely enough to achieve the goals that had been set, and the new oil sales under what was called the "food for oil" program benefited only the Iraqi elite. When Saddam Hussein expelled the U.N. weapons inspectors in 1997, not even Kuwait would support the United States in threatening Saddam Hussein with military retaliation. The coalition that had come together for Desert Shield and Desert Storm had essentially evaporated. When George W. Bush became president, inspectors still had not returned to Iraq.

THE IMPACT OF THE GULF WAR

In the United States, the Gulf War was seen by many as a military and moral victory. America had taken a stand for freedom by liberating Kuwait, and the spirit of celebration swept across the country. Americans felt that they were no longer living in the shadow of Vietnam. But American perceptions of the war did not reflect the realities of the conflict, which were quite important. Although it is always difficult to outline with precision the lessons or consequences of any war—legitimate disagreement always exists about what these might be—it is nonetheless necessary to offer some suggestions about what the possible impact of the Gulf War may have been.

After the Gulf War, it was clear that the demise of the Soviet Union would transform international affairs. As the one remaining superpower, the United States would assume new significance in the Middle East. Traditional Soviet client states such as Syria were left without reliable support and could no longer afford to oppose the United States dogmatically and consistently. Ten years after the war, Russia had almost no importance on the international scene. The United States was the clear leader in the coalition that opposed Saddam Hussein, even though disagreements among European and Arab members existed throughout the war. U.S. leadership was not a sign of its superior understanding of the region; rather, it was a reflection of its superior power and resources. After the Gulf War, nations would have to come to terms with the United States and its interests.

In January of 1991, George Bush claimed that the action against Iraq would create a "New World Order," suggesting that a new approach to collective security had emerged, but old relationships and complications remained. Even the reigning king of Jordan at the time, King Hussein, expressed his reservations about American intentions, saying that "The real purpose behind this destructive war, as proven by its scope . . . is to destroy Iraq and rearrange the area in a manner far more dangerous to our nation's present and future then the Sykes-Picot Agreement."[8] By referring to the secret agreement between Great Britain and France to divide up the Middle East after World War I, Hussein made it clear that many Arabs see the world order as essentially unchanged. From this perspective, the Soviet Union's demise has not created a new world; it has just given the United States more power. Indeed, the international coalition that opposed Saddam Hussein was fragile and transient. Almost as soon as the war ended, the combination of interests that allowed it to exist soon faded away. It took an event of the scope of the September 11, 2001, attacks on the United States to make a new international coalition possible again.

Another important consequence of the Gulf War was to impose new challenges on the traditional Arab regimes. Kuwait and Saudi Arabia were forced by circumstances to invite the United States and other modern, secular countries into their midst to protect them from aggression. Saudi Arabia now faces more serious challenges from traditional religious groups and extremist groups such as Al-Qaida, which question the regime for embracing what they identify as a source of corruption in the world. Protests by religious groups predate the Gulf War, of course. Some religious leaders, such as Sheik Hamoud al-Shuaibi, presented lists of demands after the Gulf War and were imprisoned. One of the main complaints of Osama bin Laden against the ruling elite in Saudi Arabia and the United States is that the sacred land of Saudi Arabia was defiled by the presence of American troops. Saudi Arabia is now under more pressure to sort out the relative strength that religion and secular authority will have in the future.

Saudi Arabia is also facing challenges from progressive elements in the country about increasing popular participation in the government. These concerns are not new. One of the less well-known demands of the religious radicals who took control of Mecca's Holy Mosque in 1979 was that the monarchy be abolished and replaced with an Islamic republic. The Saudi government response to the takeover of the Mosque was harsh, partly because of the concern about extreme religious groups and partly because of the challenge to the form of government.

In February of 1992, in response to concerns about the autocratic nature of the regime, King Fahd announced a series of reforms in three decrees: the Basic Statute of Government, the Statute of the Provinces, and the Statute of the Consultative Council.[9] None of the reforms was truly radical, but they were, nonetheless, significant. The Basic Statute reaffirmed the commitment of the country to Islam. The centrality of monarchy is also affirmed, but the Basic Statute announced that the rule would be defined by the sons of the kingdom's founder, Abdulaziz bin Abdulrahman al-Feisal and his grandsons. This quiet statement increased the number of princes eligible to become king from approximately 30 to over 500. The Statute of Provinces defined the responsibilities and authority of the provincial governors. The Statute created new provincial councils to advise the governors. Although members were not elected, the councils did provide new avenues for the discussion of economic issues. The councils were to include at least 10 citizens. The third decree created the Consultative Council, which has its roots in Islamic tradition. It is not an elective body and does not represent a radical turn toward democracy, but it does reflect King Fahd's desire to bring a greater number of people into the process of ruling. The king's power is not in any formal way limited by the new council, but a larger and more diverse group of advisers always has the potential of influencing policy.

The war also placed the ruling family in Kuwait under great pressure to lib-
eralize the regime. Just months before the invasion by Iraq, great political
struggles had been taking place in Kuwait over the role of a constitution and
the proper makeup of legislative bodies. Advocates of reform had been arrested as a prelude to what were controversial elections in June of 1990. After the
war, the emir had to prove to his people that the country was not returning to
the same political troubles. Kuwait felt external pressures as well. Americans
were ambivalent about fighting a war to liberate a country that did not allow its
people a significant role in governing. *New York Times* reporter Thomas Friedman said the United States should not go to war "to make the world safe for
feudalism."[10] Consequently, the emir agreed to new elections and major reforms
(see Chapter 8).

The Gulf War was in many ways a great victory for the United States, but the
victory was hollow and short-lived. Kuwait was liberated from Iraqi aggression,
but Saddam Hussein was still in power. Although his removal from power was
never a formal goal of the war, several attempts were made during bombing raids
to target his known hideouts. George Bush personalized the war by referring to
Saddam Hussein as a new Hitler bent on genocide and world domination. How
could such a man be left in power? The emphasis on Saddam Hussein as a threat
to the world made the limited military goals of the war seem insufficient. It was
awkward for the United States to go to war with a country that it had provided
with economic and military aid for so many years. The war highlighted American
confusion as much as American will.

American perceptions of the Middle East were not significantly altered by
the war. Americans were not educated about the Middle East; rather, they were
invited to cling to familiar, comfortable images. This happened in spite of the
fact that the Gulf War produced more network new stories in a shorter time than
any other event in the history of television up to that time. As many as 4,383 stories appeared on the evening newscasts during the Gulf War, totaling 126 hours
and 29 minutes of airtime. The 1988 presidential campaign only produced 2,301
stories over 22 months. By the end of the war, the Iraqi military was being portrayed as cowardly and incompetent. It was comforting for Americans who wanted to avoid complexities to hear that Iraqi soldiers were surrendering to CNN
crews. Certainly it was important for facts to be reported, but out of context these
stories and the jokes they encouraged suggested to elements of the American au-
dience who were anxious to have their prejudices confirmed that all Arabs are
threatening and yet weak at the same time. Stereotypes were not dispelled by the
press coverage of the Gulf War, and it seems unlikely that the coverage of the
War on Terrorism will produce better results.

Selected Bibliography

Karsh, Efraim, and Rautsi, Inari, *Saddam Hussein: A Political Biography* (New York: The Free Press,
    1991).

Smith, Jean, *George Bush's War* (New York: Holt, 1992).

Smith, Hedrick, *The Media and the Gulf War* (Washington, D.C.: Seven Locks Press, 1992).

Endnotes

1. Jean Edward Smith, *George Bush's War* (New York: Holt, 1992), 226.

2. John Esposito, *The Islamic Threat: Myth or Reality* (New York: Oxford University Press, 1992).

3. William Cleveland, *A History of the Modern Middle East* (Boulder, Colo.: Westview Press, 2000), 464, 469.

4. Efraim Karsh and Inari Rautsi, *Saddam Hussein: A Political Biography* (New York: The Free Press, 1991), 217.

5. Karsh and Rautsi, 245.

6. "U.S. Bombs Missed 70 percent of the Time," in the *Washington Post*, March 16, 1991, reprinted in Hedrick Smith, *The Media and the Gulf War* (Washington, D.C.: Seven Locks Press, 1992), 197.

7. Karsh and Rautsi, 251.

8. Avi Shlaim, *War and Peace in the Middle East* (New York: Penguin, 1995), 226, 136.

9. Peter Wilson and Douglas Graham, *Saudi Arabia: The Coming Storm* (Armonk, N.Y.: M.E. Sharpe, 1995), 71–74.

10. Abdo Baaklini, Guilain Denoeux, and Robert Springborg, *Legislative Politics in the Arab World: The Resurgence of Democratic Institutions* (Boulder, Colo.: Lynne Rienner, 1999), 187.

Chapter 3

The Power of Stereotypes

A story is told about John Foster Dulles, the U.S. Secretary of State in the 1950s. When he was asked what could bring peace in the Middle East, he said: "Well, what we need is for the Jews and the Arabs to start treating each other in a Christian manner."[1] Whether or not this story is a fair representation of Dulles's attitudes, it does reflect a common view that people who are unfamiliar to us are somehow defective. Muslims, who are often identified solely as Arabs, and Jews are not well understood in the United States because they have always been a small minority. Most Americans do not form their opinions about them from personal experiences; rather, they depend on portrayals of them in literature, the news, or in the popular media as substitutes for firsthand knowledge.

Approximately 2 percent of the population of the United States is Jewish and approximately 2 percent is Muslim (figures vary). Once one leaves the major cities (where the minority population can be a much higher percentage), the percentage of the Muslims and Jews to the total population is even smaller, and it is not uncommon for many people to have never met a Muslim or a Jew. In spite of this, few Americans lack some picture in their minds of what Muslims and Jews are like. Walter Lippman argued in a classic work on media images that stereotypic thinking "precedes reason," and "as a form of perception [it] imposes a certain character on the data of our senses."[2]

Misconceptions about these two minority religious groups ultimately affect the way in which the United States conducts both its foreign and domestic policy. Popular images of Muslims and Jews can make or break diplomatic initiatives and encourage or discourage military action in times of crisis. "The media images in our heads," argues Michael Parenti, "influence how we appraise a host of social realities, including our government's domestic and foreign policies."[3] If we have "learned" from the media (either the news or the entertainment media) that Muslims or Jews are hostile or dishonest, then we are likely to offer our support to governmental policies that address these perceptions of reality.

We draw on deeply felt stereotypes when we confront world affairs. For example, after the September 11, 2001, terrorist attacks on the World Trade Center and the Pentagon, many Americans viewed Islam as a religion of terrorism. Muslims were perceived as terrorists, in spite of a number of public statements by President

George W. Bush urging Americans to distinguish between Islam and terrorism. Bush attempted to make it clear that the war on terrorism that he was launching was not an assault on Islam, but on those who perverted Islam for their own political purposes. Bush gave a speech emphasizing that American Muslims "love their flag as much as other Americans do," but since the terrorists who hijacked the planes that were used in the September 11 attacks did identify themselves as Muslims, the image of Muslim as terrorist was strengthened. This stereotype was enhanced by late night talk shows, where jokes were made about the word Allah, where Muslims were ridiculed for wearing beards, and where Islam was linked directly to a love of camels, the oppression of women, and a hatred of everything Western.

For weeks following the September 11 attacks, Muslims around the United States were harassed (attacks against Jews also increased, especially in Europe). Bullets ripped through the windows of mosques and bricks with obscene death threats were thrown though the windows of Arab Americans. In Alexandria, Virginia, an Islamic bookstore had two bricks thrown through its windows with notes tied to them. The first note said "Arab Murderers" and the second began with an obscenity and then said "You come to this country and kill. You must die as well."[4] After September 11, women wearing head scarves were insulted on the streets, and men who looked "Middle Eastern" were threatened. The power of these stereotypes is revealed by the report from a Sikh religious organization that several hundred of their followers were harassed in the weeks following September 11 simply because they wear turbans and some of them have dark skin. Sikhs are a reformed Hindu group that originated in East Punjab, India. One Sikh was shot in Arizona because someone thought he looked like an Arab or a Muslim. By mid-November, 2001, the American Arab Anti-Discrimination Committee had confirmed 520 violent acts committed against Arab Americans. In addition, there were almost 30 incidents where people perceived as "Middle Eastern" were expelled from aircraft without any cause (in spite of the fact that the Department of Transportation has stressed that this kind of discrimination is not only "immoral but illegal"). In spite of the Bush administration's clear statements in support of Islam and law-abiding Arabs, the Justice Department embarked on an aggressive policy of questioning Muslims and Arabs in the country about possible ties to terrorist organizations, raising questions about whether religious or ethnic profiling was behind the government's investigations.[5] At the same time, some groups in the United States stood by Muslims and Arabs and led prayer meetings and multiculturalism meetings to combat the dangerous tendencies of these stereotypes. Even in times of crisis, not all succumb to the temptations of stereotyping.

The word "stereotype" is derived from the language of journalism. The first stereotype was called a flong, which was a printing plate that made it possible to reproduce material. The typesetter could use the flong to avoid recasting type.[6] Drawing on the original understanding of the word, one could define a stereotype as an image one uses in order to avoid the trouble of analyzing facts and making subtle distinctions. Most people depend on stereotypes in their day-to-day affairs as a kind of shortcut in the thinking process. Parenti points out that Americans sometimes exclaim that something is "just like in the movies." When this happens, they are "expressing recognition and even satisfaction that our media-created mental frames find corroboration in the real world."[7] People often focus their attention on matters of primary concern and deal in stereotypes for other matters. Stereotyping takes place in the news media as well as in the entertainment media, and both manifestations can create serious problems for Muslims and Jews. When stereotypes appear in the news media, they are harmful because people want to believe that the news media exists to inform them about the facts. Even if they have a healthy skepticism about what they hear on the news, they may not apply that skepticism to the stereotypes themselves. Movies can also have a profound effect on attitudes. Parenti points out that even though we consciously know that a particular movie or television program is fictional, "we still 'believe' it to some extent; that is, we still accumulate impressions that lead to beliefs about the real world." When people attempt to think about social and political issues, they draw on the images in their heads. "We do not keep our store of media imagery distinct and separate from our store of real-world imagery."[8]

Stereotypes are not the only barriers to understanding among people; prejudice is a more deeply rooted attitude and may not be susceptible to correction by the introduction of better information or communication. In other words, some people hate others even though they understand them quite well.[9] But stereotypes are a significant social problem, and Muslims and Jews are two groups that have been victims of stereotyping throughout American history.

STEREOTYPES OF MUSLIMS

Images of the Muslim have gone through three different stages in American history. Muslims have, at different times, been known as: (1) mysterious, (2) incompetent, and (3) violent. These different images cannot be confined strictly to different periods—the images overlap—but there has been a general transformation over time. Until the mid–1960s Muslims were rarely in the news, literature, or movies and television. They did not make up a significant enough proportion of the population to be noticed, and they were not perceived to be important enough to average Americans to play a role in film. One popular image of the Muslim appeared in the movie *Lawrence of Arabia*, based on the book *The Seven Pillars of Wisdom*, written by T.E. Lawrence. The movie portrays the Arab revolt against the Ottoman Empire during World War I. T.E. Lawrence was the British officer who worked with the Arab forces and who decided to dress like them and live with them during the conflict. Lawrence developed real affection for the people he came to know, but the view he presents of his Arab and Muslim friends is often condescending. According to his account and the British interpretation of his involvement in the Arab revolt, Lawrence was its leader. The movie version allowed American audiences an opportunity to enter an unfamiliar world, led by a familiar figure: a British officer. Arabia was unknown to most Americans, and yet romantic, with gallant men on camels fighting for a cause endorsed by the West. In some ways, this film introduction to Arabia is reminiscent of the film introduction to Africa provided by Tarzan movies, which featured vast, beautiful territory with strange but interesting natives, once again led by an

Englishman. Film critic Roger Ebert comments in his review of the movie that part of its appeal is that it features the desert. "For a moment we experience some of the actual vastness of the desert and its unforgiving harshness." He suggests that unconventional characters and the mood of the movie are important reasons for its success:

> I've noticed that when people remember *Lawrence of Arabia,* they don't talk about the details of the plot. They get a certain look in their eyes, as if they are remembering the whole experience, and have never quite been able to put it into words.[10]

In *Lawrence of Arabia* the actor Omar Sharif, himself a convert to Islam, plays the part of Ali, who is a strong, mysterious tribesman who lives by a solemn code. The Muslims in this movie, represented by Sharif, are admirable in some ways; Ali is driven by pride and a passion for freedom, but what he values and how he responds to the world is odd. Ali at one point kills Lawrence's guide for violating tribal rules and drinking at his desert well. Sharif became "a sort of generic exotic heartthrob" partly as a result of the character he played in this movie.[11]

Lawrence of Arabia was released in 1962, before the Arab-Israeli conflict had captured the American imagination. The second stage in the development of the Muslim image begins only a few years later, after the 1967 Arab-Israeli war. Building on stereotypes already in existence, the American view of the Muslim changed. Now the Muslim was incompetent, not exotic and romantic. The 1967 war became known as the Six-Day War, where a tiny Israel under attack by a vast, united Arab army was able to defeat its enemy with seeming ease. Even though Israel had a superior military force at the time, most Americans saw Israel as the underdog and were impressed by the Israelis and perplexed by the Arab defeat. Edmund Ghareeb confirms this: "Israel is portrayed as the fledgling state surrounded by incompetent but threatening neighbors who outnumber the tiny state ten-fold."[12] The only way for many Americans to explain the Israeli victory was to see the Muslim as unskilled and perhaps cowardly. During this period, Muslims are usually identified as Arabs. The dashing figure of Omar Sharif is replaced by the image of Egyptian or Syrian soldiers fleeing an Israeli advance on the battlefield.

The third stage in the development of the Muslim image in America began in 1973, when the Arab oil embargo was imposed on the United States. A sense of fear and vulnerability spread across the country as people had to face gas rationing. Americans were angry, partly because they were worried about the supply of oil and partly because it seemed wrong for Muslims to have any real power in the world. The word "blackmail" was used to describe the embargo. Some journalists spoke out against this attitude. William Raspberry wrote:

> Why is it "diplomacy" when the United States uses national resources as a leverage in its foreign policy and "blackmail" when the Arabs do the same thing? We hear the Arab oil embargo described so frequently and so matter of factly as blackmail that we start to take it as undisputed fact. But when American wheat or American technology is withheld in order to influence the diplomatic postures of other countries, it seems the most reasonable thing in the world. Why the inconsistency?[13]

Throughout the oil embargo, the word Arab continued to be used to describe the enemy. Of course, OPEC includes countries like Iran, which is largely Muslim but not Arab, and countries such as Venezuela and Nigeria as well. Arabs and Muslims became almost synonymous in the popular arts. Movies like *Black Sunday* portrayed Arabs as bloodthirsty terrorists who are willing to detonate a bomb in a blimp over a football stadium during the Superbowl. Arabs are seen here as threatening what many would consider to be the heart of American life: football.[14]

Negative images of Muslims increased after 1979, when the American embassy in Iran was overrun by students and its employees were taken hostage. From the perspective of most Americans, the Shah of Iran had been a modern ally, and the Muslims who followed the Ayatollah Khomeini were anti-Western extremists. Articles began to appear in the press and on television identifying the Muslim with anti-Americanism and violence. Khomeini stated explicitly that it was his goal to export his revolution throughout the world, and Americans began to think of Islam as a challenge to the West in the way that communism had been perceived in the 1950s. The term "Islamic Fundamentalist" became popular in the decade following Khomeini's revolution in Iran, and many Americans began to view all Muslims as violent fanatics. The Arnold Schwarzenegger movie *True Lies* depended upon generic Arab/Muslim extremists for its story of nuclear arms theft. The Denzel Washington movie *The Siege* also presented powerful images of a Muslim willing to kill thousands of innocent people in the name of his religion.[15] The stereotype of the violent Muslim continues to dominate popular perceptions of Islam in the United States. Today, that image may make it difficult for many Americans to understand the problems faced by Muslims throughout the world. With regard to the Middle East, such an image could make it difficult for Americans to distinguish Islam from terrorism.

STEREOTYPES OF JEWS

Jews have been better known than Muslims in America, since Christianity understands itself as developing out of Judaism. Perceptions of Jews initially came from the religious tradition. Popular media built on these perceptions and developed the powerful stereotypes that exist today. Three basic images have emerged: (1) the Jew as stubborn; (2) the Jew as tricky; and (3) the Jew as wealthy and powerful. Together, these images have placed real barriers between Jews and the Christian majority in the United States. These images have an impact on the way in which the majority of Americans view the tensions in the Middle East.

The idea of Jewish stubbornness has its roots in old, religious criticisms of Jews. In 1654, a small group of Jews arrived in New Amsterdam (later called New York) and asked for permission to settle in the New World. Although they were later admitted, the governor of New Amsterdam, Peter Stuyvesant hoped to deny the request on the ground that Jews are "hateful enemies and blasphemers of the name of Christ."[16] He believed that Americans should be suspicious of Jews because they stubbornly refused to accept Jesus as the messiah, even though the evidence for his divinity was overwhelming. The idea of Jewish stubbornness often manifests itself as general disapproval of Jews for being troublemakers. In 1879, the president of the Manhattan Beach Corporation explained why he was establishing a policy of banning Jews from Coney Island:

> Personally, I am opposed to Jews. They are a pretentious class who expect three times
> as much for their money as other people. They give us more trouble on our
> [rail]road and in our hotel than we can stand. Another thing is that they are driving
> away the class of people who are beginning to make Coney Island the most fashion-
> able and magnificent watering place in the world.[17]

Jews have a bad attitude. They cause trouble and make life unpleasant for decent
people. This is the message he presents. These complaints are connected more
to class than religion; their roots are often forgotten.

The image of the Jew as tricky also plays a powerful role in the American
consciousness. In the years between the two World Wars, Jews were often excluded from consideration for jobs because of questions about their character. In a
speech to Harvard Law School, the head of an important New York law firm explained his exclusionary hiring practices:

> Brilliant intellectual powers are not essential. Too much imagination, too much wit,
> too great cleverness, too facile fluency, if not leavened by a sound sense of propor-
> tion, are quite as likely to impede success as to promote it. The best clients are apt to
> be afraid of those qualities. They want as their counsel a man who is primarily honest,
> safe, sound and steady.[18]

Jews are intelligent, but tricky. Their dishonesty is offensive to the "right" kind of
people. Jews are to be feared because of their drive and intelligence, since it may
be in the service of dishonest goals.

The image of the Jew as wealthy and powerful became popular in the United
States in the post-Civil War period, when the forces of industrialization left rural
America economically depressed. Populist demagogues often pointed their fingers at the Jews, suggesting that they were behind the farmers' troubles. In 1895,
an article appeared in *Illustrated America:*

> Might it not be that the money lenders of London, the magnificent, titled Shylocks of
> our modern world, who play with Czars, Emperors and Kings as a chess-player with
> castles, rooks and pawns, in the artificial production of a panic . . . may have pur-
> posely wrought the ruin of many American banks . . . because in America these gam-
> blers of the banking world reap their richest harvest and wish to continue their
> tightest grip on the people?[19]

These same themes were adopted by Henry Ford, who opened up a detective
agency to investigate what he perceived to be pernicious Jewish activities and
published the *Dearborn Independent,* which was almost exclusively devoted to attacks against what he believed were the secret plots of Jews to control American
politics and society through "Jew finance." This was also a time of vicious charac-
terizations of Jews in cartoons. As John Appel has pointed out, characters such as
the big-nosed, calculating, money-mad Hockheimers, Diamondsheens, and Bur-
nupskis were popular in the media.[20]

Contemporary portrayals of Jews in the popular media perpetuate these
stereotypes. In his movie *Mo' Better Blues,* Spike Lee presents the character of the
Jewish agent as dark and sinister, motivated by a desire for money and willing to
destroy the close friendships of his African-American clients in order to serve his

interests. One of the most pernicious images presented in literature and film is that of the affluent Jewish woman, known as the Jewish American Princess, or JAP. The 1969 movie *Goodbye Columbus* presents a negative picture of the suburban Jewish family and especially of the daughter. Marshal Woodbury points out that the JAP is a "stereotype of an overindulged daughter of a newly prosperous suburban Jew. As with any nouveau riche, the immigrant Jewish family would lack the social skills to go with its new wealth."[21] In other words, Jews don't really belong in the upper classes. A Jewish family may achieve some kind of economic success, but it will never develop the "proper" attitudes. Woodbury points out that at some colleges, such as Cornell, in the past students have worn T-shirts that say "SLAP-A-JAP" and "BACK OFF BITCH, I'M A JAP-BUSTER." At Syracuse University, graffiti announced: "A Solution to the JAP Problem: When they go to get nose jobs, tie their tubes as well." These crude and offensive statements present Jews as uneasy and awkward among "mainstream" Americans.

Today, the image of the wealthy, powerful Jew who cannot be trusted is part of American politics. Former Vice President Spiro Agnew wrote a novel entitled *The Canfield Decision* in which there is a secret plot by Jews in the American press attempt to use their positions of power to promote Zionism. What is especially disturbing about the book is that its conspiracy theory thesis was being offered by a major political figure, not a right-wing extremist. More recently, this same theme figured prominently in speeches of presidential candidate Pat Buchanan. In his criticisms of U.S. involvement in the Gulf War, he described the United States Congress as "Israeli-occupied territory." He suggested that Jews supported the war, but wanted the fighting to be done by "kids with names like McAllister, Murphy, Gonzales, and Leroy Brown."[22] In other words, Jews are wealthy and powerful, but cowardly. They are directed by a foreign power, Israel, and are tricky enough to avoid actual fighting themselves.

The dominant images of Muslims and Jews in America suggest that Muslims are linked to violence and that Jews use their wealth and power to manipulate world affairs. Since American foreign policy ultimately depends on popular support for its long-term effectiveness, these negative images can have an impact on the way in which the United States approaches the Middle East.

IGNORANCE AND THE MEDIA

One important reason that stereotypes of Muslims and Jews are powerful in the United States is that media coverage of the Middle East is generally poor. Edward Said argues in *Covering Islam* that many reporters are ignorant of the region and some do not even know the languages of the people in the countries to which they have been assigned. Few reporters speak Arabic, but even in Israel, where many residents speak English, not knowing Hebrew can be a problem. During the years when Begin was prime minister, reporters consistently underestimated his political support, often predicting that he would not last in office. This was the perspective of the reporters who spent their time with college-educated Israelis who spoke English and tended to be opponents of Begin. These reporters had no easy access to the Jews who spoke Hebrew or French and were the backbone of

---

Two Anti-Defamation Groups

1. The Anti-Defamation League. This Jewish organization was founded in 1913 by lawyer Sigmund Livingston. Its mission was "to stop, by appeals to reason and conscience, and if necessary, by appeals to law, the defamation of the Jewish people . . . to secure justice and fair treatment to all citizens alike . . . put an end forever to unjust and unfair discrimination against and ridicule of any sect or body of citizens." The ADL monitors hate crimes and acts of discrimination around the country. It also provides information about bias in the media. You can learn about the ADL through its web page at [www.adl.org].
2. The American Arab Anti-Discrimination Committee. This American Arab organization is designed to defend the rights and "promote the rich cultural heritage" of people of Arab descent. It was founded in 1980 by former Senator James Abourezk. It works to combat negative stereotyping of American Arabs and to promote a "more balanced U.S. Middle East policy." It also serves as a resource for the media and for community activities. Its Department of Legal Services also works through the courts to defend the civil rights of American Arabs. You can learn about the ADC through its web page at [www.adc.org].

---

the Likud Party. Of course, being knowledgeable about the region is ultimately more important than speaking the languages, but many reporters lack even a basic education about the Middle East. For example, a reporter from a major U.S. newspaper recently revealed his ignorance by asking whether Jerusalem was located on the Mediterranean or the Red Sea; since geography is important to any report on tensions in the Middle East, not knowing this fact is serious.

The news media need to get their stories out quickly, and this also creates problems. After the takeover of the American embassy in Iran in 1979, stories ran suggesting that the PLO was behind the action. Marvin Kalb reported on CBS *Nightly News* that the PLO was responsible for mining the compound. This was thought to be evident because "the sounds of Arabic" could be heard inside the embassy.[23] The story was completely incorrect; there was no evidence then or now that the PLO was involved, and the fact that Arabic was heard inside the embassy is completely irrelevant. Many Muslims speak Arabic and many pray in Arabic. A story like this obviously needed to be researched more fully before it was reported, but the pressures on the media to release stories quickly in order to stay ahead of the competition leads to serious errors.

Another example of this same problem is from the Fall of 2000, during street conflicts between Palestinians and Israelis. The American media was embarrassed when it released a picture taken by an Israeli journalist. The picture depicted a young man covered with blood next to an Israeli soldier holding a stick. When American reporters received the picture, they could not read the comments of the Israeli journalist, since they were in Hebrew, and they simply assumed—under the pressure of the moment—that the young man was a Palestinian who was being beaten by the Israeli soldier. The violence taking place between Israeli security forces and Palestinian crowds backed by the Palestinian police had yielded so many sad and frightening images that the American media believed the photographs were easy to interpret. The *New York Times* printed the picture with a caption that matched the assumptions of the media, only to discover that the young man was an American Jew being rescued from violence by the soldier. The *Times* also misrepresented the place of the attack, identifying it as the Temple Mount, even though a gas station was clearly in the background of the picture. The need to get the story out quickly meant that the media depended upon assumptions and perceptions, not facts.[24]

Harmful images of Muslims and Jews continue to permeate the American media because they have, for one reason or another, not been able to rise to the challenge of reporting with the depth of understanding necessary for complex issues and diverse people. Edward Said argues that most of the knowledge we have of other people is "unscientific," but that this can be overcome if two conditions are fulfilled. First, anyone approaching a study of the Middle East must be "answerable to and in uncoercive contact with the culture and the people being studied." In other words, one must really know the way of life and the people about whom you wish to report, and this knowledge cannot be derived from tainted sources. Secondly, interpretation of people and their ways is often dependent upon a historical situation. "No interpretation can neglect this situation, and no interpretation is complete without an interpretation of the situation."[25] Certainly, it would be a mistake to suggest that all stories are merely the result of interpretation, but it is quite reasonable to take account of the power of an historical situation to color most interpretation. Reports about the Middle East often suffer from the passions and prejudices of their particular historical situation. Muslims and Jews will often be presented as representing evil forces in the world if the biases of the historical situation allow for it.

The problem with our perceptions is not just the fault of the media. Few Americans know much about the non-American media. After the September 11 attacks on the World Trade Center and the Pentagon, many Americans heard about the Arab satellite network (owned by the government of Qatar) *al-Jazeera*. It is the channel that Osama bin Laden used to send his videotaped messages to the world. But this network is not really watched by many; only about 10 percent of Arabs in the region own satellite dishes, and those who watch *al-Jazeera* tend to be critical of it. Even the Bush administration seemed to be unaware that other media are more popular and more highly regarded. A number of important administration officials, including Secretary of State Colin Powell, Secretary of Defense Donald Rumsfeld, and National Security Adviser Condoleezza Rice, granted interviews with *al-Jazeera* and turned down opportunities to be interviewed by newspapers such as *Asharq Al-Awsat, Al-Hayat* (both based in London), and *Al-Ahram* (based in Cairo). After their own national TV networks, many Arabs turn to the BBC World Service, the French government's Radio Monte Carlo, and Egyptian Radio. Radio is especially important to some countries like the Sudan, where many do not own televisions. The most popular and well-respected satellite news services are the Middle East Broadcasting Corp. (MBC),

Abu Dhabi TV, Orbit TV, and Egyptian TV.[26] Most Americans can gain access to a number of English versions of newspapers and magazines in the Middle East through the Internet. If we can become better informed, then it is less likely that our politics will be so dominated by stereotypes.

In his classic work *The Image,* historian Daniel Boorstin discusses the artificial world created by the media, and he warns that Americans are threatened by "the menace of unreality." He says that "We risk being the first people in history to have been able to make their illusions so vivid, so persuasive, so 'realistic,' that [we] can live by them."[27] Yet Boorstin cautions his readers against simply pointing their fingers at the media as being responsible for the current situation. "While we have given others great power to deceive us . . . they could not have done so without our collaboration." The stereotypes of Muslims and Jews that continue to appear in the media are there at least in part because they match the expectations of the majority of Americans. Ultimately, the media is not the enemy; our own willingness to accept stereotypes helps to mold the forces that in turn present us with images of the world in which we live.

Selected Bibliography

Boorstin, Daniel, *The Image: A Guide to Pseudo-Events in America* (N.Y.: Atheneum, 1971).

Ghareeb, Edmund, *Split Vision: The Portrayal of Arabs in the American Media* (Washington, D.C.: American-Arab Affairs Council, 1983).

Parenti, Michael, *Make-Believe Media* (New York: St. Martin's Press, 1992).

Endnotes

1. Ze'ev Chafets, *Double Vision: How the Press Distorts America's View of the Middle East* (New York: William Morrow, 1985), 27. Chafets acknowledges that the story might be apocryphal, but he suggests that it accurately reflects the attitude of many in American politics.

2. Walter Lippman, *The Image.*

3. Michael Parenti, *Make-Believe Media* (New York: St. Martin's Press, 1992), 4.

4. *Washington Post National Weekly Edition,* vol. 18, no. 47, September 17–23, 2001, 31.

5. ADC Fact Sheet: The Condition of Arab Americans Post 9/11, www.adc.org.

6. Willard F. Enteman, "Stereotyping, Prejudice, and Discrimination," in *Images that Injure,* Paul Lester, ed. (Westport, Conn.: Praeger Publishers, 1996), 9.

7. Michael Parenti, *Make-Believe Media* (New York: St. Martin's Press, 1992), 4.

8. Parenti, 7.

9. See "Stereotypes and Prejudice: Their Automatic and Controlled Components," by Patricia G. Devine, in *The Journal of Personality and Social Psychology,* January 1989, vol. 56, no. 1, 5–18.

10. Roger Ebert, *Roger Ebert's Video Companion* (Kansas City: Andrews and McMeel, 1996), 856.

11. "Arab Americans: Middle East Conflicts Hit Home" in *Images that Injure,* 65.

12. Edmund Ghareeb, *Split Vision: The Portrayal of Arabs in the American Media* (Washington, D.C.: American-Arab Affairs Council, 1983), 6.

13. Edmund Ghareeb, 7.

14. See Parenti, 30.

15. The movie also included a subplot that attacked prejudice against Arabs and Muslims. This adds to the complexity of the movie and places it above many others that link Islam and violence, but the major thrust of the movie in many ways obscures the subplot.

16. "Antisemitism in the United States: A Historical Perspective," by Jack Wertheimer, in Jerome A. Chanes, *Antisemitism in America Today* (New York: Carol Publishing Group, 1995), 34.

17. Wertheimer, 44.

18. Wertheimer, 48.

19. Wertheimer, 40.

20. John Appel, professor of American Thought at Michigan State University points this out in *Ethnic Images in Comics*, Museum of Balch Institute for Ethnic Studies.

21. "Jewish Images that Injure," by Marsha Woodbury in *Images that Injure,* 50.

22. Wertheimer, 52.

23. Said, 81.

24. A correction was printed in *the New York Times,* October 7, 2000.

25. Said, 155–156.

26. Mamoun Fandy, "The Proper Channels," *The Washington Post: National Weekly Edition,* December 10–16, 2001: vol. 19, no. 7, 22.

27. Daniel Boorstin, *The Image: A Guide to Pseudo-Events in America* (New York: Atheneum, 1971), 240.

Chapter 4

The Legacy of Imperialism

The past weighs heavily on the Middle East in a way that many in the West find difficult to understand. This issue emerged recently when President Bush began to discuss his plans to combat terrorism after the September 11, 2001, attacks. His first remarks referred to the planned War on Terrorism as a crusade. He did not understand that the wounds from the Crusades are still felt in the Middle East. Once advisers informed him of the emotional response produced by the word, Bush chose different ways to characterize his War on Terrorism. Like the Crusades, imperialism has left its mark on the Middle East, adding complexities to contemporary conflicts in ways that are sometimes difficult to perceive.

Imperialism is difficult to define because it is a complex phenomenon and because it is a political term often used for polemical purposes. One traditional definition is that imperialism describes a "relationship of effective domination or control, political or economic, direct or indirect, of one nation over another."[1] Imperialism is often identified with the actions of European powers in the nineteenth century, but it can be traced back as far as the Greek and Roman empires and is probably as old as the political community itself. Clearly, forms of imperialism exist today. Imperial domination, as Ronald Chilcote points out, implies that a nation has lost either its sovereignty or its autonomy. This can happen as the result of direct and open intervention, diplomatic advantage, or economic means.[2] While a loss of sovereignty is easily identified, autonomy can be lost in ways not immediately evident or verifiable. For example, one country can undermine the social mores or religious traditions of another country. The scholar A.P. Thornton explains that one motive for imperialism was the desire to change the way of life in subject countries: "Imperialism is a policy forced upon a civilised [sic] nation by the very fact of its civilisation."[3] The imperial powers believed that the countries they controlled were being given the gift of civilization. Thornton identifies the imperialist perspective that favored social and religious transformation of what were considered to be inferior people: "Such races were unable, not having the knowledge, to maintain a civilised rule themselves. Such a rule it was the duty of a civilised nation to provide, and therefore the government of dependencies was a necessity in the modern world."[4] In other words, imperialism can involve military action, domination by treaty, or economic domination, and it is often accompanied by a belief that some nations are the bearers of civilization to the world. Imperial powers often hope that their way of life will transform the countries they dominate.

THE OTTOMAN EMPIRE

Western powers began to take an active interest in the Middle East when it became clear that the Ottoman Empire was in decline, so any attempt to understand the Middle East must include a discussion of the Ottoman Empire, one of the great powers in the history of the world. The term "Ottoman" is the European form of Uthman, the name for the family dynasty that came to power in 1280 in the area we now call Turkey.[5] In 1453 the Ottomans conquered Constantinople and within a hundred years had extended their influence well into Europe, controlling Greece, Hungary, the area around the Black Sea, Serbia, Bosnia and Herzegovina. In the East, the Ottomans took control of Egypt, Palestine, Syria, Arabia, and Iraq. In other words, at the height of its power, the Ottomans ruled from the heart of Europe to the Persian Gulf. This was a blow to the Arabs, who lost political independence to the Turks when the Ottomans took control. The new rulers imposed the Turkish language on the Empire for all matters of official business and encouraged new literature and art that was designed to glorify the new way. The Ottomans introduced their own version of imperialism, long before the Europeans became powerful in the Middle East.

As Emory Bogle points out, "The Ottoman Empire was not a nation, but a federation of different peoples and regions, which were spread over an immense area under differing degrees of control by the sultan and his government, the Porte."[6] In other words, the people under Ottoman rule were, in fact, subjects, but they identified themselves by reference to tribe or locality. Ottoman rule allowed a certain amount of local autonomy for the great number of peoples under its authority, including Kurds, Greeks, Druze, Jews, and Christians.[7] Non-Muslims were ruled as *dhimmis,* subject peoples who were protected in return for special taxes and obedience to special laws. Bogle says that since the empire was never very efficient, some could obtain limited independence, except in cases of rebellion or failure to pay taxes. Since the Middle East included large, underpopulated areas, Arab independence from Ottoman control was maintained by default in places where the government did not reach. In the cities and in large population centers, Arab rule ended.[8]

The center of power for the empire was the sultan, who ruled in accordance with *sharia*, or Muslim law. He controlled the military, filled offices according to his pleasure, and issued ruling decrees. There were no formal, structural limitations on the sultan's powers, but he could not ignore the ruling family, the bureaucracy, the military, or religious leaders.[9] In the sixteenth century, the sultan also took on the title of caliph, in order to assume ruling authority in Islam. The government was administered on behalf of the sultan by a council, under the leadership of the grand vizier. The empire was divided into *millets*, which were religious communities administered by the leader or executive council, according to the dictates of their religions. Only Muslims were subject to *sharia.* The *millets* collected taxes and organized courts of law.[10] Decentralization was characteristic of Ottoman rule.

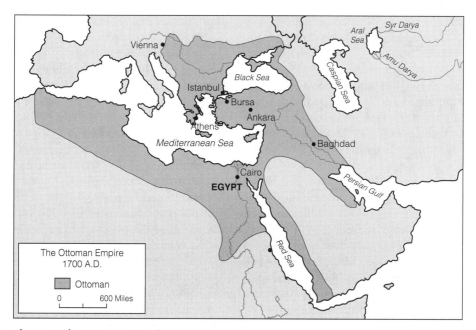

Figure 4 The Ottoman Empire

The empire faced a multitude of challenges as it attempted to rule the enormous area under its control. In order to address the financial burdens of rule, special treaties were made with foreign governments such as France to encourage commercial activity. These treaties reduced tariffs, granted navigation privileges, and guaranteed that merchants would not be subject to Muslim law. These treaties were known as capitulations, which referred to the word for "chapter" in the treaties. Too many concessions were made in these treaties, and the empire gave up too much power over economic activities. In addition to economic problems, corruption within the government weakened the Porte (a term used to describe the government of the sultan, since power came from the palace gate), and the military went into decline when its elite Janissaries warriors were allowed to marry. The growing weakness of the empire came to the world's attention in 1683, when it attacked Vienna and was opposed by Polish forces who saw themselves as defending Christianity against the infidel. The Turks were defeated in a great battle that left over 10,000 dead.

The Ottoman Empire never regained its former glory. The decline of the empire over the next 200 years and the maneuverings of other countries to benefit from its demise are often identified as "The Eastern Question."[11] A competition developed between European powers and Russia for the area that had been under Ottoman rule. Initially, Russia took the lead in defeating Ottoman forces and gaining control of new land, including long-desired access to the Black Sea. This, in turn, disturbed the British, who were worried that Russian successes would threaten their interests in the East. The French became involved in the

Middle East in 1798 when Napoleon sent approximately 40,000 troops to Egypt to try to disrupt British communications with India. Ultimately his troops advanced through what was then known as Palestine and into Syria, challenging Ottoman control of the region. Napoleon's campaign could not be sustained; the British fought back, and Napoleon's troops returned to France by 1801, but the campaign had a great impact on the region. First, it established links between Egypt and France, and second, it compelled the British to focus more attention on the Middle East.[12] It also demonstrated to the world that the Ottoman Empire was vulnerable to attack.

In order to survive, the Ottoman Empire attempted to play the British and French against the Russians, but European reservations about the authoritarian character of Ottoman rule led to a period of liberalization designed to win the favor of the West. This period is called the *Tanzimat*, or Reorganization period, which lasted from the 1830s until 1876. During this time, the government sought to reverse its traditional policies based on decentralization and to seek stronger control over the provinces, something seen as necessary for increasing tax revenues. The promised reform was quite radical and included a plan to recognize equal treatment of all Ottoman subjects, to reform the tax system, and to require a fair trial in cases that involved capital punishment. It also established a Council of Judicial Ordinances, which was designed to pass legislation for the approval of the sultan.[13]

The radical character of the reforms made them difficult to accomplish without deep social changes. The reforms therefore were eventually seen to depend upon changes in education, which in many ways aggravated the problems of the empire by raising expectations in the general population. The old religious schools were supplemented by a new system of secular schools, and school was made mandatory for boys. European printing presses were introduced to the empire to address the needs of the rising number of readers, and in 1832, the first Turkish newspaper was established.[14] The reforms were generally perceived as failures and created widespread resentments. Even those who were in sympathy with the idea of reform were critical of the way in which the reforms were being carried out. A group known as the Young Ottomans criticized the government for continuing to be authoritarian and demanded that a new constitution be established to curb the power of government. In response to these concerns and rising economic problems, a constitution was put into place in 1876, but it did not accomplish all that the Young Ottomans hoped for. Within two years, the parliament was dismissed and the constitution continued in name only.

The weakening of the empire created new opportunities for challenges to Ottoman rule from within. Muhammad Ali (1769–1849), known as the founder of modern Egypt, was an Albanian who first came to Egypt with the military force that was sent in 1801 to drive Napoleon out of the region. After the French were driven out, he destroyed the power of the Mamluks and was appointed the Pasha of Egypt by the sultan in 1805. His power increased until he came into direct conflict with the Porte over his claim to Syria. In 1831 he sent troops to Syria under the authority of his son and succeeded in defeating the Ottoman army. The sultan was forced to place Syria under Muhammad Ali's control. The embarrassing defeat of Ottoman forces prompted the sultan to turn to Russia in 1833 for protection from what he perceived to be Egyptian ambitions.[15] This, of course, alarmed the British, who hoped to benefit from growing Ottoman weakness.

They sponsored a European blockade of Syria, which succeeded in driving Muhammad Ali's forces out of Syria and forced him to return control of the land to the sultan. The major European powers had won a temporary victory over Russia for control of the declining empire.

Egypt prospered under Muhammad Ali's rule, partly because of his determination to emulate European ways. He brought in French advisers to modernize his military and worked to build schools and medical facilities.[16] He sent Egyptian students to study in Europe. Bogle says that "Young Egyptians, thus, became familiar with European ideas, technology, and institutions far sooner than their surrounding Arab brethren."[17] As Brown says, he "was probably more responsible than any other individual for accelerating the pace of direct European involvement in the Middle East."[18] He even attempted to develop a modern manufacturing industry, although this endeavor was not terribly successful. Muhammad Ali's challenge from within to Ottoman power contributed to the rise of Egypt, but it also created conditions that encouraged outside powers to increase their efforts to gain control of the empire.

Muhammad Ali died in 1849, and Egypt once again went into decline under the rule of his descendants. In 1856, the French obtained permission to build a canal that would connect the Mediterranean Sea with the Red Sea. Egyptian labor was used for the project, and partial ownership was offered to Egypt's ruler in return for his cooperation. Egypt found itself in the position of granting European concessions like the canal, which were designed to help the economy in the long run, but which allowed European powers increasing influence over the country's affairs. As the Egyptian economy worsened, the British government purchased the Egyptian shares in the canal. This gave the British an excuse to send forces into Egypt in 1882 when a revolt broke out. This military action was followed by British occupation of Egypt that lasted until 1956.

THE MIDDLE EAST AND WORLD WAR I

When Germany declared war on Russia in August of 1914, the Ottoman Empire, which had developed a close relationship with Germany over the years, entered the war on Germany's side. The British wanted to strengthen their presence in the Middle East, so they declared Egypt a British protectorate in December of that same year. Also, British forces landed in Iraq to secure the oil fields. During the war, regional Arab leaders began to approach the British to try to secure some independence. At the same time, Jewish leaders also hoping for independence approached the British for their support. The two most well-known products of these negotiations stand in a kind of tension. The first is the Hussein/McMahan correspondence and the second is the Balfour Declaration. Together, they are symbols of the damage and confusion that European imperialism caused in the region.

Hussein, the sharif of Mecca (and the great-grandfather of the recent King of Jordan) engaged in communication in 1915 and 1916 with Sir Henry McMahon, Britain's high commissioner in Egypt.[19] Letters between the two led Hussein to believe that the British would support his hope of reviving the caliphate through Arab independence in the area. The most important of these letters said that

Britain was ready "to recognize and support the independence of the Arabs in all the regions within the limits demanded by the Sherif [namely, the entire Arab rectangle, including Syria, Arabia, and Mesopotamia]," excluding the "portions of Syria lying to the west of the districts of Damascus, Homs, Hama, and Aleppo." Note that the wording in the letter is vague. Different people had different interpretations of what the "districts" were that were referred to in the letter. Since all the lands discussed were in flux, detailing excluded areas was technically impossible. All the lands under consideration were still under the control of the Ottoman Empire. The letter along with the others made it clear that Arab support in the war against the Ottoman Empire was the price to be paid for independence. This was the foundational understanding that led to the Arab revolt in 1916 under the leadership of the Emir Feisal, Hussein's second son. The famous T. E. Lawrence, known as Lawrence of Arabia, was dispatched by the British to assist Feisal. Lawrence, who worked closely with a number of Arab leaders, but most importantly with Feisal, was taken into the confidence of his fellow warriors in the Arab revolt. But Lawrence knew before the revolt was very far along that the British had no intention of honoring their promises to Feisal. In spite of this, he continued to act as if he were a friend to the Arabs. He did develop strong ties with Feisal and others, but in the end, Lawrence supported the British war aims.

The reason that Britain excluded several areas from the agreement with Hussein is that it was also involved in delicate negotiations with France over the fate of the region. In 1916, Sir Mark Sykes and Charles Francois Georges-Picot concluded an agreement for postwar control of the area. Britain would oversee Arab land in Mesopotamia, Transjordan, and southern Palestine. France would have authority over southern Turkey, Syria, northern Palestine, and part of upper Mesopotamia. The divided interest in Palestine led to conflicting understandings, even though there were complicated attempts to outline ways in which both countries could retain some control over some parts of Palestine. But by the time the agreement had been signed, the British were already having misgivings about it. In order to protect the Suez Canal, Britain felt that it should control Palestine as well. Britain began to look for a way out of its agreement, and the Jews seemed to be the answer to the problems the British were facing. When a new prime minister and foreign secretary came into power, England was ready to move in a new direction. As Sachar points out:

> The movement of decisive reappraisal in Middle Eastern policy came in the last weeks of 1916, when Lloyd George and Balfour became prime minister and foreign secretary, respectively. As the new government recognized, the Sykes-Picot Agreement no longer was a sufficiently watertight guarantee for British interests in Palestine. Perhaps, then, the Jews as a client people might be as useful an opening wedge for British domination as were the Arabs.[20]

Neither the Jews nor the Arabs had any interest in being "client people," but from the perspective of the British, this was the goal. As Sykes said, "a prosperous Jewish population in Palestine, owing its inception and its opportunity of development to British policy, might be an invaluable asset as a defense of the Suez Canal against attack from the north and as a station on the future air routes to the East."[21] Yet, for some time, leading Jews in England had been talking about their desire to return to what had been their country in ancient times and where they had always maintained a presence. This movement, known as Zionism, received a favorable hearing in England (see Chapter 6).

The most famous zionist in England during World War I was Dr. Chaim Weizmann, a chemistry professor at the University of Manchester. He was not aware of the strategic issues that colored the British reception to his recommendations any more than Hussein was aware of the weak support for real Arab independence. He pursued his dream and eventually developed a relationship with some leading English politicians. Finally, a letter of support was sent from the British government to the head of the British Zionist Federation in November of 1917:

> His Majesty's Government view with favour the establishment in Palestine of a national home for the Jewish people, and will use their best endeavours to facilitate the achievement of this object, it being clearly understood that nothing shall be done which may prejudice the civil and religious rights of existing non-Jewish communities in Palestine, or the rights and political status enjoyed by Jews in any other country.[22]

Note that this declaration is vague, just as was the Hussein/McMahon correspondence. What is a "national home"? Is it a country with independence or is it a housing project under foreign rule? Even more importantly, what is Palestine? At the time, the name Palestine comprised what is today known as Israel, Jordan, and part of Syria. Most at the time assumed that an independent state was envisioned, but as British enthusiasm for this project declined, the wording of the declaration allowed for a number of British retreats.

Like the Arabs, the Jews were recruited to join in the fighting. A Jewish legion was created by the British and served in the final campaign of the war against the Ottoman Empire. By the time the war ended, the Jewish legion had 5,000 soldiers, which was one-sixth the size of the British occupation force and about half the size of Arab forces under Feisal at the time.[23]

THE MANDATE PERIOD

When the war ended, a series of agreements transformed the Middle East. A peace agreement was signed in Paris in 1919, but the terms for the control of the Middle East were not concluded until the San Remo Conference in 1920, where Britain and France divided up the lands formerly under Ottoman rule. The League of Nations endorsed this intrusion of European power, calling the action mandated by the postwar conditions in the area. Mandates were "inhabited by peoples not yet able to stand by themselves under the strenuous conditions of the modern world." The European powers, therefore, were given the responsibility of ruling "until such time as they are able to stand alone." Despite the exalted language, Cleveland argues:

> By phrasing the matter in this way, the league attempted to gloss over the fact that mandates were simply another name for imperial control. The mandate system provided Britain and France with an opportunity to secure their strategic interests in the Middle East while paying lip service to the widely publicized principle of self-determination.[24]

The League of Nations assigned Syria to France and Iraq and Palestine to Great Britain. The mandate system stood in direct conflict with Arab and Jewish hopes of independence. By 1920, Feisal had already begun to form what he hoped would be an independent Syrian nation with him as king, but he was thwarted by the French, who sent troops into Damascus and crushed Feisal's forces easily. This move also nullified the will of the Syrian congress that Abdullah, Feisal's brother, be made king of Iraq. At the Peace Conference in 1919, France had assured the Sunni Muslims in Syria that it would not use its mandate to divide the region, but by 1920 Syria had been divided into pieces, creating an independent Lebanon, Damascus, and Aleppo, and the districts of Latakia, Jabal Druze, and Alexandretta. As Daniel Pipes said, "the divisions were clearly an attempt to exploit ethnic and religious differences."[25] In other words, the French believed that the area would be easier to dominate if the different people were set against one another. It was committed to Christian control of Lebanon under the Maronites, which frustrated the Muslim population and laid the foundation for tensions that played a major role in Lebanese politics through the 1980s.

These actions, of course, were in direct contradiction with the idea of the mandate, which was to encourage the development of independent rule. Instead, the French maintained control of all high administrative positions and set up obstacles to the authority of local officials. The French actions finally led to a major revolt in Jabal Druze in 1925, which the French felt compelled to end through the use of massive force. By the end of the conflict two years later, thousands were dead and thousands were homeless. The tensions continued during World War II, even after the Vichy administration was replaced by De Gaulle's. Even after the war ended, the French continued to resort to force to eliminate local opposition to its authority. Finally, in 1946, the French reluctantly withdrew from Lebanon and Syria, leaving the area scarred by its presence.

The British were equally clumsy with their mandate. Churchill became colonial secretary in 1921, and his main adviser was T.E. Lawrence. Churchill decided to advance British interests in the area by placing into power men over whom he believed the British could exert decisive influence. He gave Iraq to Feisal after the French evicted him from Syria. Britain used its influence to manufacture an artificial referendum supporting Feisal (after arresting one of the other candidates and convincing others to withdraw).[26] The Iraq given to Feisal was drawn by the British without any consideration for the indigenous people. The Kurds, for example, were not consulted when the creation of modern Iraq out of two Ottoman provinces and Mosul undermined the Treaty of Sevres, a 1920 treaty that seemed to promise an independent state to the Kurds. Of course, the problem of the Kurds continues to this day, informing policy in Iraq and Iran, not to mention Turkey. Kuwait was chopped up into pieces, disappointing the emerging Iraq, in order to compensate Ibn Saud, the sultan of the Najd for the loss of territory to Iraq. Churchill, who has justly earned American honor for his role as prime minister in fighting the Nazis, seemed to care little about the people whose fate he sealed with what can only be called an arrogant and callous foreign policy in the Middle East.

Churchill also gave control of a new nation to Feisal's brother, Abdullah. The nation of Transjordan was created in 1922, and it consisted of about 75–80 percent of the land that had formerly been called Palestine, which the Jews had thought was promised to them by the Balfour Declaration. This was, in effect, a major modification of the declaration, which Churchill's famous White Paper issued in 1922 made clear. The White Paper stated the British had never really intended to support an independent Jewish state. It also limited Jewish immigration to what was left of Palestine in order to appease growing Arab fears. An additional problem was that Abdullah had not been chosen by any people to be a ruler, and he had no direct ties to the area that was created by the British. He was clearly installed as a British puppet. In return for being given a nation to rule, Abdullah would receive a monthly subsidy from England, advisers to help him administer his territory, and a vague promise of independence for the future.[27] Transjordan would not become independent until 1946.

Arabia was not placed under the League of Nations mandate, and it developed its own character through the efforts of Ibn Saud, a warrior who led through the authority of the Wahhabi movement within Islam. Wahhabism originated with Mohammad al-Wahhab, who promoted a conservative Islam in the 1720s. The emerging country enhanced its legitimacy by serving as the protector of Muslim holy sites. As he became more powerful in the region, the British worked through treaties to maintain their interests. Meanwhile, the Americans wanted to expand their involvement in Arabia, now called Saudi Arabia, primarily to explore for oil. The Standard Oil Company had no trouble securing the right to drill for oil; Ibn Saud had few economic alternatives available. Saudi Arabia was neutral for most of World War II, but the country cooperated with the Allies. In spite of this alliance, Ibn Saud developed a country with real independence.

The British suffered under their mandate, as did the people they dominated. Tensions between Jews and Arabs rose in Palestine, and both resented the British presence. Jews focused on organizing emigration, and the Palestine Zionist Executive came into existence in 1921. Under its new name, The Jewish Agency, it created a semiautonomous assembly that was granted limited power by the British. Arabs created a congress of their own in 1919, but it was not an effective organization and was replaced by the power of the Supreme Muslim Council, under the leadership of Hajj Amin.[28] Arab emigration to Palestine also increased at this time. Jews worked to purchase land in Palestine, believing that this was an appropriate method of settlement. However, many Arabs resented the sales and challenged their legitimacy. Violence began to break out between Jews and Arabs, and the British worked to maintain order and placate the two groups. One response of the British was to limit Jewish immigration to Palestine, but this was poorly timed because Hitler's rise in Germany had only increased Jewish interest in Palestine. Just before the invasion of Poland in 1939, the British were forced to send 20,000 troops to Palestine to deal with fighting there. During World War II, violence between Jews and Arabs escalated, and both groups attacked the British. In 1947, the United Nations became involved again, recommending the partition of what remained of Palestine (following the creation of Transjordan) into separate Jewish and Arab states. The partition plan was reluctantly accepted by the Jews, but the Arabs felt they had been betrayed by the international community. Attacks and counterattacks plunged Palestine into confusion. Finally, in 1948, the British left Palestine in frustration without resolving any of the conflicts that divided the people.

Britain and France had tried to create a region that would bend to its will after World War I; instead, they managed to establish a network of resentments and to lay the groundwork for a host of conflicts that were destined to follow. In a remarkably penetrating statement on this issue, Shlaim says

> In the war's aftermath, they [Britain and its allies] refashioned the Middle East in their own image, building a new political and territorial order on the ruins of the old. They created states, they nominated persons to govern them, and they laid down frontiers between them. But most of the new states were weak and unstable, the rulers lacked legitimacy, and the frontiers were arbitrary, illogical, and unjust, giving rise to powerful irredentist tendencies.[29]

The mandate system lasted from the end of World War I to the period just after World War II. France and Britain had every reason to think they were laying the groundwork for long-term possession of the Middle East, but their direct control faded away in a few years. Imperialism as a force did not disappear, and the actions of the French and British changed the area forever, but both imperial powers were forced to retreat from their positions of authority and look for other ways to pursue their national interests.

The age of traditional imperialism is over, but the world seems unable to avoid involvement in the Middle East. It remains a major focal point for international action. World War I inspired the old imperial powers to impose themselves on the region, but their influence declined significantly by the end of World War II. For the 50 years following, the Cold War defined superpower action in the Middle East.

During the great era of superpower competition, the United States and the Soviet Union thought of the world as a kind of stage upon which their great rivalry would be played out. From their perspective, the most important world events were those relating directly to their interests. American foreign policy was informed at this time by the policy of containment. Since many believed that the superpowers were too dangerous to challenge each other directly, the United States developed a strategy to challenge Soviet attempts at expansionism around the globe in a series of small conflicts. The rationale for containment was first articulated by George F. Kennan, who wrote

> that the main element of any United States policy toward the Soviet Union must be that of a long-term, patient but firm and vigilant containment of Russian expansive tendencies. . . . Soviet pressure against the free institutions of the Western world is something that can be contained by the adroit and vigilant application of counterforce at a series of constantly shifting geographical and political points.[30]

One implication of this strategy was that all world events were seen from the perspective of this struggle. It therefore became important to the United States to attempt to counter any increase of Soviet influence wherever it emerged. One of the unfortunate results of this policy of containment is that during this era the United States offered its support to a number of authoritarian rulers who used this support to oppress their own people. For example, the United States played a significant role in bringing the Shah of Iran into power (see Chapter 1). We saw him as Western-leaning and therefore worthy of our support. As Mackey has pointed out, "the United States enlisted the shah as an ally against the rising power of Stalinist Russia."[31] The Shah used American interest in Iran to bolster his hold on power. But his regime was cruel, and when he was finally driven from power in 1979 by those supporting the Ayatollah Khomeini, it was natural for the people of Iran to see the United States as an enemy. Americans had swarmed over Iran in pursuit of their own interest, completely insensitive to the impact they were having on the country. "Americans ignored the dual threat to Iran's values and cultural identity posed by Muhammad Reza Shah's reach for absolute power."[32] In other words, one of the side effects of containment was that it put the United States into the position of using countries in ways that were not good for their people in order to pursue its global concerns. This is clearly not traditional imperialism; the United States manipulated Iranian politics in order to prevent what it thought to be dangerous for the entire world: increased Soviet power. The United States believed that it was doing the right thing for the world, and yet the policy of containment led to a kind of tunnel vision.

During the 1980s, the United States increased its support for Israel and what it considered to be Western-leaning Arab states, including Lebanon, Jordan, Egypt, and Saudi Arabia. It was hoped that this would counter Soviet influence in Syria, Iraq, and the PLO. Concern about superpower conflict also informed the U.S. perspective on negotiations between Israel and the Arab states for peace. It is extremely important to see that the United States saw negotiations in the Middle East as part of a larger picture. The United States supported the kinds of negotiations and the kind of peace that would be best for what it perceived to be the superpower conflict. What did the Soviets want? Where would they invest their influence next? These were the questions U.S. diplomats asked themselves.

In many ways, the superpower involvement in the Middle East resembles the old-style imperialism of England and France. Clearly, a sense of superiority pervaded U.S. policy. Why should U.S. policy makers listen carefully to the views of the people in the Middle East? How could they possibly know how important their region is to world peace? They are concerned with themselves, not the world. The policy of containment is well-intentioned, but narrow. Like classic imperialism, the policies pursued by the United States were about a vision of the future world. The United States was not immune to considerations of self-interest, but the superpower conflict was about the destiny of the world, not self-interest narrowly understood. Concern with peace in the Middle East was linked to the U.S. hope that the Soviet Union would not dominate the world. Regardless of whether or not policy makers in the United States correctly understood the Soviet Union, their decisions about foreign policy were informed by that understanding. This was evident during the Reagan administration. As Quandt puts it, "Reagan placed primary emphasis on the Soviet threat to the Middle East, not on the Arab-Israeli dispute," especially at the beginning of his term in office.[33] He and his Secretary of State, Alexander M. Haig, Jr., worked to develop a "strategic consensus" among what were called the moderate states. The theory was that countries in the region would deemphasize their differences once they became convinced that they held in common a desire to defend themselves from Soviet aggression. Reagan therefore pursued a policy of supplying arms to pro-Western states.

Classic imperialism was about imposing a way of life on what were thought to be backward people. The British believed they could instruct what were essentially children in lessons of civilization. This meant, among other things, that the British believed that Christianity was superior to Judaism and Islam. Containment was about ideas as well. However, the United States saw itself as the country with the power to promote freedom and equality, principles it believed were denied by the Soviets. The Soviets wanted to lead the world in new directions and presented an alternative to capitalism they truly believed would be better for the world. Classic imperial powers looked down on the people they dominated, and the superpowers did the same thing, but their ultimate goals were different.

The superpowers were focused on their own problems partly because they possessed nuclear weapons, and they felt an awesome responsibility for the future of the world. In other words, their ability to destroy the world gave them the sense that the world was theirs to manipulate. What could be more important than the survival of the globe? The petty concerns of those in the Middle East had to be seen as distractions from the main issue: How can nuclear war be prevented? One has to admit that there is some force to this perspective, but it is quite limited. Yet the amazingly destructive power of nuclear weapons was difficult to ignore. Once the Soviet Union disintegrated and the threat of comprehensive nuclear war disappeared, the United States remained the sole, surviving superpower. It remains to be seen if the United States can develop an approach to the Middle East that reflects a deeper understanding of the region.

American policy makers have generally believed that they understand the Middle East better than it understands itself. At best, this attitude manifested itself as a tendency on the part of American presidents to lecture or chide leaders from the Middle East. American presidents generally believed that Arabs and Israelis were too close to their own troubles to see the big picture. Americans approached leaders from the region in the way that tolerant parents might approach squabbling children. For example, when President Carter first met with Israeli Prime Minister Rabin in 1977, he opened serious discussions with a "harsh injunction to Rabin to forget about the past and adopt a fresh attitude."[34] This lecture revealed a real naïveté about the Middle East in the form of an American pragmatism divorced from the sensitivities of the past. A more subtle form of this arrogance is the belief that American peace plans always reflect the best hope for the future and that disagreement with an American plan reflects an obstructionist attitude.

Classic imperialism and its intrusive modern manifestations have been real obstacles to the search for peace in the Middle East. The region is important to the world for strategic, religious, and economic reasons, but outside powers have given the people there only modest opportunities to address their problems without outside interference. In an increasingly global political environment, no part of the world can or should hope to exist in isolation, but the history of the Middle East makes it especially sensitive to the involvement of international actors.

Selected Bibliography

Bogle, Emory, *The Modern Middle East: From Imperialism to Freedom: 1800–1958* (Upper Saddle River, N.J.: Prentice Hall, 1996).

Brown, Carl, *International Politics and the Middle East: Old Rules, Dangerous Game* (Princeton, N.J.: Princeton University Press, 1984).

Cohen, Benjamin, *The Question of Imperialism: The Political Economy of Dominance and Dependence* (New York: Basic Books, 1973).

Endnotes

1. Benjamin Cohen, *The Question of Imperialism: The Political Economy of Dominance and Dependence* (New York: Basic Books, 1973), 15.

2. Ronald Chilcote, *Theories of Comparative Politics: The Search for a Paradigm Reconsidered* (Boulder, Colo.: Westview Press, 1994), 251. My discussion of imperialism draws heavily from this thoughtful and complex work.

3. A.P. Thornton, *The Imperial Idea and Its Enemies* (New York: Doubleday, 1959), 86.

4. Thornton, 86.

5. Brown, 26.

6. Emory Bogle, *The Modern Middle East: From Imperialism to Freedom, 1800–1958* (Upper Saddle River, N.J.: Prentice Hall, 1996), 4. The gateway to the buildings that held the council of the grand vizier became known as the High Gate or Grand Porte, and Porte became the name for the government.

7. Jason Goodwin, *Lords of the Horizons: A History of the Ottoman Empire* (New York: Henry Holt, 1998), 91. Goodwin says that "the very nature of the territory they inherited made it vital that people looked after themselves: it was one thing to marshal armies at a whistle and send them thundering up the border roads, quite another to penetrate into every nook and cranny of this remarkably corrugated empire and attend to all that was going on."

8. Bernard Lewis, *The Arabs in History* (New York: Oxford Univesity Press, 1994), 174.

9. Helen Chapin Metz, *Turkey: A Country Study* (Washington, D.C.: Library of Congress, 1996), 20.

10. Bogle, 5.

11. George Lenczowski, *The Middle East in World Affairs* (Ithaca, N.Y.: Cornell University Press, 1980), 32.

12. L. Carl Brown, *International Politics and the Middle East: Old Rules, Dangerous Game* (Princeton, N.J.: Princeton University Press, 1984), 25. Brown says that "after Napoleon's military venture to the Eastern Mediterranean, British statesmen never ceased worrying about the lifeline to India."

13. Bogle, 23.

14. Bogle, 18.

15. Lenczowski, 38.

16. Bogle, 12.

17. Bogle, 12.

18. Brown, 43.

19. Walter Laqueur and Barry Rubin, *The Israel-Arab Reader: A Documentary History of the Middle East Conflict* (New York: Viking Penguin, 1984), 15. See also Shalaimi, 12 and Sachar, 92.

20. See the thoughtful and clear treatment of this in Sachar, 97. My discussion owes most of its insights to this analysis.

21. Sachar, 100.

22. Sachar, 109.

23. Howard M. Sachar, *A History of Israel* (New York: Knopf, 1991), 114–115.

24. Cleveland, 170.

25. Daniel Pipes, *Greater Syria* (New York: Oxford University Press, 1990), 29.

26. Shlaim, 12–13. This discussion of postwar power-brokering is quite thorough.

27. Sachar, 126.

28. Cleveland, 248.

29. Avi Shlaim, *War and Peace in the Middle East* (New York: Penguin Books, 1995), 17.

30. George F. Kennan, "The Sources of Soviet Conduct," in *Foreign Affairs,* July 1947.

31. Sandra Mackey, *The Iranians* (New York: Plume/Penguin, 1996), 240.

32. Mackey, 240.

33. William Quandt, *Camp David: Peacemaking and Politics* (Washington, D.C.: The Brookings Institution, 1986), 18.

34. Quandt, 45. These are Quandt's words, but they describe the tenor of the meeting.

Chapter 5

The Rise of Arab Nationalism

In order to understand the clash of aspirations that has fueled the Arab-Israeli conflict and many other developments in the Middle East, it is important to understand both Arab and Jewish nationalism. As Chapter 4 has shown, imperial powers were actively involved in the Middle East at the time when both Arab and Jewish nationalism were becoming significant forces. Both have played a role in the political landscape of the Middle East, but they have also contributed to the way in which Arabs and Jews understand themselves. The development of this self-understanding is as important as the more specifically political effects of nationalism.

Rashid Khalidi defines Arab nationalism as "the idea that Arabs are a people linked by special bonds of language and history (and many would add, religion), and that their political organization should in some way reflect this reality."[1] There are two main schools of thought that attempt to explain the rise of Arab nationalism. The traditional explanation, represented by authors such as George Antonius, is that contact with the West inspired nationalism, that Arabs developed a new interest in self-determination because of their new contact with secular Western ideas. This view presents Arabs as importing lessons from Western politics, and it suggests that the great Arab national movements were not derived from their own independent thought and action. Arab nationalism is seen here as a reflection of European nationalism. Elie Kedourie begins with this basic perspective and then suggests that Arab nationalism was essentially established by the military officers who were placed in power by the British after World War I. It was only later that Arabs began to invest this Western movement with meaning and to link it with Islam.

A newer, revisionist perspective is offered by people like C. Ernest Dawn, and although it has also been subjected to scholarly criticism, it's basic perspective is still dominant today.[2] Dawn argues that Arab nationalism was a form of protest by Arab elites in Syria against Ottoman rule, and that it had its roots in Islamic modernism. According to this argument, imitating the West was undesirable because it, in effect, presented Islam as a failure, and while it was destructive to see Islam as a failure, it was clear to most Arabs by the end of the

59

nineteenth century that Muslim rule in the Ottoman Empire was, in fact, a failure. Dawn argues:

> The cure for the present humiliation and abasement of the Muslims was to return to the true Islam of their ancestors. This done, the power and glory that Islam had lost to the Christian West would return to its rightful owners. That the true Islam was the Islam of their ancestors, and the ancestors were Arab, meant the revival of Arabism and the Arab culture and the restoration of the Arabs to their position of leadership among the Muslims.[3]

Muhammad Rishid Rida, a Syrian author who moved to Egypt in 1897, was one of the representatives of Islamic modernism. He wrote that Muslims were weak because they had turned away from the basic truths of Islam. He believed that the strength of the Europeans was a secular strength, but that Arabs could remain true to Islam without rejecting modern science and politics.

Another important figure was Abd al-Rahman al-Kawakibi, also a Syrian who moved to Egypt. He was one of the important contributors to Islamic modernism. His two books, *Characteristics of Tyranny* and *Mecca: Mother of Cities,* argue that the Ottoman Empire had become despotic and had turned away from true Islam. The corruptions of the empire had affected all aspects of life for the people under its control. Only Arabs could be trusted to bring about the changes needed. Islam, he argued, needed an Arab caliph with spiritual duties only, except in the Hijaz, where some temporal responsibilities would be necessary. He believed that the new caliph should be chosen from the family of the Prophet and from the Arabian peninsula, where Islam had maintained its purity. As Bogle comments, "this was unquestionably an Arab-nationalist, even Pan-Arabist, position. It ascribed a moral, and perhaps intellectual, superiority of Arabs over Turks."[4]

THE ARAB REVOLT

The most important expression of early Arab nationalism was the Arab Revolt of 1916.[5] This revolt set the stage for the Sharif Hussein's establishment of a kingdom in Syria and for his later rule in Iraq. The birth of Transjordan was an indirect result of Hussein's activities. The Arab Revolt marked a crucial stage in Arab opposition to Zionism because it elicited promises from the British that, in the eyes of Arab nationalists, involved Arab control of Palestine. Yet, as William Ochsenwald points out, the Arab Revolt was an "ironic beginning" because it took place in a part of the Ottoman Empire that was not at all nationalistic. Hussein's main goals seem to have been more religious than political, and they do not seem to have been based on ethnic, Arab identity. The emerging theories of Arab nationalism that were very much alive in Syria and Egypt did not have strong, vocal representatives in the Hijaz. (The Hijaz or "Barrier" is the western land in Arabia, containing the coastal strip and the highlands. It includes the two holy cities.) Ochsenwald argues that the majority of the Hijazis, who lived in towns, "were reasonably happy with the Ottoman-amirate government." This satisfaction was derived from a tradition of limited Ottoman control, gifts of grain and money from the empire, protection from crime, and respect for Islam. The nomads from the countryside were generally unhappy with the empire, but their unhappiness did not produce any kind of movement. One thing that both the townspeople and the nomads agreed on was that the Hijaz should maintain a semiautonomous Hijaz.[6] In other words, Ottoman rule was accepted, as long as it was basically profitable and not too intrusive.

Leaders such as 'Awn al-Rafiq worked to resist the centralization of Ottoman power, which was symbolized by the building of the Hijaz Railroad. The railroad was designed to be a new line of communication with the empire. Sharif Hussein also opposed the railroad, and before he was appointed amir in 1908, he participated in attacks on the railroad as it approached Medina. He and others managed to keep the railroad from reaching Mecca, but Medina suffered. Authority was taken away from local leaders and the city was administered directly by the Ottoman government. However, resistance to Ottoman power was not in the name of nationalism; rather, it was inspired by a desire to preserve local privileges and the special religious status of the Hijaz in the empire. Ochsenwald shows that the professional groups that were so instrumental in developing nationalistic ideas in Syria and Egypt were not in the Hijaz. Since there was no conscription into the army in the Hijaz, no elite military corps with an Arab identity was developed. The only printing press in the region in 1908 was owned by the Ottoman government.[7]

According to Ochsenwald, the ruling authority in Istanbul, the Committee of Union and Progress, let Hussein know that if he continued to oppose the railroad, he would be deposed. This is when Hussein began to reach out to nationalists in Syria and to the British in Cairo. "If the autonomy of Mecca was to come under direct assault, as seemed likely, Hussein hoped to turn to one or the other group for help."[8] When World War I broke out and the Ottoman Empire supported Germany, the delicate status of the Hijaz was threatened. Hussein could no longer depend on the empire for safety, supply routes might be cut off, and at the same time that it was losing control, the empire toughened its policies in the provinces. Istanbul prepared for increased centralization of power over the Hijaz, which is exactly what Hussein wanted to avoid. An independent Arab state became even more attractive under these circumstances.

Some independent newspapers began to surface after 1908, including Al-Islah al-Hijazi, which Hussein supported financially. Owned by a Syrian, it published articles from the Egyptian press. Although the newspapers did not stay in business for very long, they succeeded in introducing a number of controversial issues that had become important elsewhere in the Arab world. Some reforms in the Ottoman educational system also encouraged new thinking that was in opposition to Ottoman interests, but the vast majority of Arabs in the Hijaz were not nationalists; the ideas were too new and did not permeate the region by the beginning of the very revolt that in many ways defines Arab nationalism. As Ochsenwald put it, "Arab national independence began in the nonnationalistic Hijaz."[9]

The circumstances of the war encouraged Hussein to take independent action to protect the religious sites and his religious authority, and his contacts with the Syrians and British led him to present his goals in religious and increasingly nationalistic terms. Hussein's son, Abdullah, had begun meetings with Lord Kitchener in Cairo to see if the British might support independence in the Hijaz. Abdullah told British representatives on behalf of his father that "the people of the Hijaz will accept and be well-satisfied with more close union with Great Britain . . . , owing to the notorious neglect by Constantinople of religion and its rights . . . Great Britain will take first place in their eyes so long as she protects the rights of our country . . . and its independence."[10] Hussein's son, Feisal, had been spending time in Syria, and returned from Damascus with plans drawn up by radical nationalist societies for an independent Arab nation. Mary Wilson points out that the British also began to speak with Abdullah about "the Arab nation" and "the emancipation of the Arabs." Wilson suggests that Hussein spoke to the British in terms that they would understand; he "chose an idiom that was especially comprehensible to European sensibilities."[11] One thing is clear, the language of nationalism was in place by the time that Hussein began his famous negotiations with Sir Henry McMahon in July of 1915. At the same time, Hussein presented his goals to the people at home in mainly religious terms. In a letter to McMahon, Hussein spoke of the "Arab nation" and its desire to "gain its freedom," and yet the newspapers in Mecca argued that the Ottoman Empire had launched "an attack on Islam," and charged that the leaders in Istanbul "do not care about religion or the *sharia* . . . and have begun to live under the signs of apostasy and unbelief."[12]

The causes of the Arab revolt will continue to be the subject for serious study. Was the revolt inspired by the religious motives of Hussein? Was the nationalism of the revolt taught to Hussein by his contacts with Syrian thought? Or was it contact with the British that ultimately defined the revolt in nationalistic terms? If it was contact with the British that defined the revolt as a nationalistic struggle, was it because Hussein learned nationalism from the British, or did he simply use the language of nationalism in order to appeal to an imperial force in terms it would understand?

THE DRIVE TO PAN-ARABISM

Arab hopes of independence and nationhood were crushed by the imposition of European control over the Middle East after World War I. The mandates began in April of 1920 and, as Bogle says, "provided Arab nationalists with a greater challenge than the Ottomans had presented."[13] Nationalist movements seemed from this point on rather petty if they did not address the overwhelming fact of European domination. A movement began to redefine Arab nationalism in terms of the unity of all Arab people under one rule, rather than the cooperation of a number of different, independent Arab states. One of the early proponents of what became known as Pan-Arabism was Sati al-Husri, who was the dean of the Law School at the University of Baghdad. As Reeva S. Simon has pointed out, he developed a theoretical foundation for the movement based on his study of Germany.[14] He stressed the importance of language in developing national identity and argued that Arab leaders should cease supporting small, regional states. Arabs constituted one nation and should seek a single, all-comprehensive state.[15]

The first movement to rise from these new theories was the Baath (Resurrection) movement in Syria, which became important in the 1940s. Deborah Gerner states that "the Ba'th Party is one of the only political movements that is truly indigenous to the Arab world."[16] It was founded by two Syrians, Michael Aflaq, a Greek Orthodox Christian, and Salah al-Din al-Bitar, and merged with the Arab Socialist Party in 1953 as it broadened its support from intellectuals to become a large-scale movement. Its motto was "One Arab Nation, One Immortal

Mission." The party was devoted to pursuing economic and social justice through Arab socialism. Aflaq, however, did not fashion the party's principles on the models of either capitalism or communism; he charted what he believed was a distinctive path. In addition to socialism, the party stood for opposition to imperialism and Zionism (which it considered to be a form of imperialism). The party hoped to bring together Muslims and non-Muslims in a political structure organized under Arab-Islamic principles. This meant, of course, the complete abolition of all existing states in the Middle East and their replacement by a single Arab state under the control of the Baath Party.

The party had an uncompromising character, which manifested itself as an unwillingness to work with other groups. Consequently, most of its work in the early years was done in secret. Members did not, generally speaking, know who belonged to the party or who was truly important within the party structure. This contributed to the growth of the party, and yet in some ways kept the party from achieving elective success. It was not until the 1950s that the party was even willing to compromise enough on its principles to allow cooperation with elements within the military in Arab states that were sympathetic to the party's goals.

The Baath Party became especially influential in Syria and Iraq, and was one important force behind the political union of Syria and Egypt in 1958. This union, known as the United Arab Republic, was not successful as the national goals of the two countries failed to give way. In 1961, Syria forcibly ejected Egypt's representatives and the U.A.R. was dissolved. Within a few years, the Baath Party in Syria split into two factions, and in 1966 a military coup supported by one of the factions was successful, laying the foundation for the 1970 coup that culminated in the ascension to power of Hafez al-Assad, who ruled until his death in 1999. In Iraq, the Baath Party had a stormy history, sometimes exercising power and sometimes being out of favor with those in power. The 1958 revolution was supported by the Baath Party, but it was not strong enough to force Iraq into joining the U.A.R. Saddam Hussein became a member of the Baath Party in 1957, only to flee the country in 1959 after he failed to assassinate the president of Iraq. Hussein spent several years in Cairo, returning in 1963, when the Baath Party seized power in Iraq. Unfortunately for Hussein, the Baath government was overthrown the next year and he was imprisoned. He became the deputy secretary general for the Baath Party while he was in jail, and helped to organize activities in secret until the revolution of 1968 brought the party back into power. By the 1970s, the Baath Party was of central importance to every aspect of Iraqi society; even the officer corp of the military was placed under the control of the party, which was responsible for promotions. In 1979, all members of the ruling council of the Baath Party became members of the Revolutionary Command Council (R.C.C.), and the distinction between the party and the State was essentially eliminated.[17] Saddam Hussein took over power that year after appointing himself a general.

NASSER AND PAN-ARABISM

Gamal Abdel Nasser was born on January 5, 1918, into an Egyptian family of modest means. His father was a post office clerk and his mother was the daughter of a businessman. Nasser was interested in social change from the time he was

17 years old and was arrested several times for participating in student riots. He entered the army in 1938, fighting in the Sudan and against Israel. He was also the member of a murder squad that plotted political assassinations.[18] He took a leading role in organizing the Free Officers, a group of about 400 officers, most of which were under the rank of major. This was the group behind the 1952 military coup in Egypt that overthrew King Farouk. Nasser was in power as president by 1954 and was courted by members of the Baath Party, who hoped to recruit him to their Pan-Arabist goals, even though Egypt in many ways had not traditionally thought of itself as an Arab country.

Nasser was drawn to a number of leftist movements, including the Baath Party, but his approach to politics, at least in the early years, was more pragmatic than theoretical. In his book *The Philosophy of the Revolution,* Nasser comments that he believed the Free Officers were a vanguard of the people and that after the revolution all would be united in Egypt as one. But this did not happen, and factions fought each other violently, vying for power. Nasser admits that he really had no long-term plan of action. He was disappointed that the country seemed divided and the people were at each other's throats. As he says, "Personal and persistent selfishness was the rule of the day. The word 'I' was on every tongue."[19] Nasser urged Egyptians to unite in order to complete the revolution the army had begun, and he offered imperialism as the enemy:

> . . . Imperialism is the great force that throws around the whole region a fatal siege. I thus began to believe after these facts became established within me, in one common struggle and repeated to myself, "As long as the region is one, and its conditions, its problems and its future, and even the enemy are the same, however different are the masks that the enemy covers its face with, why should we dissipate our efforts?"[20]

As Malcolm Kerr points out, Nasser's connection with the military suggested his general approach. He and the other graduates of the Egyptian military academy "approached specific ills in a pragmatic spirit with whatever means came to hand."

> Their initial ideology, to the extent they had one at all, was primitive and general: they were against corruption, social oppression, and imperialism, and they proposed to clean up the country, strengthen the army, build up the economy, broaden opportunities for the lower classes, and—when they were ready—institute a 'clean' democracy.[21]

This group of military officers distrusted political parties—and the Baath Party was primarily a political party. All political parties in Egypt were therefore dissolved and replaced by a mass organization known as the Liberation Rally, which had no real power in the face of the Revolutionary Command Council.

The Baath Party in Syria seemed to support many of the same goals that Nasser was fighting for in Egypt, and this led to the experiment in union, the U.A.R. But the differences between the two countries were too significant; Nasser hoped to dominate the union, and this was resented by the leaders of the Baath Party in Syria. After the breakup of the union, Nasser sought to define the problem without abandoning his view that all Arabs should be united. Nasser argued that belief in the ultimate merging of all Arabs was more important than the transitory cooperation of existing Arab governments, especially when they are dominated by reactionary forces. A unity of goals, he asserted, was more important than a unity of governments:

> Unanimity over purposes is more important than unity of ranks. We call for unity of purpose, but we look with suspicion on slogans calling for unity of ranks. Unity of ranks based on different purposes would drive the entire Arab nation into danger . . . It would mean we set little store on our aspirations . . . We seek to achieve unity of purpose in the first place. Such unity can lead to unity of ranks, because unity of purpose constitutes unity of all the Arab peoples. All the Arab peoples have one and the same goal, but certain rulers are working toward different goals.[22]

Kerr argues that from 1960 on, Nasser's approach to Pan-Arabism was reminiscent of Stalin's "socialism in one country." The idea was to move toward the desired goal by focusing temporarily on development within one country. Nasser offered a sense of destiny and historic inevitability, according to Kerr, to Pan-Arabism while at the same time drawing attention to divisions in the Arab world. Nasser attempted unsuccessfully to link this specifically Egyptian form of nationalism with religion. He felt it was necessary to make use of religious symbols. He nationalized al-Azhar University, a respected Islamic institution, and he used a state magazine, *The Pulpit of Islam,* to draw connections between Arab nationalism and Islam. However, the nationalistic movement was based on the idea that solidarity was defined by common language and history, and while it did not reject Islam, it was primarily a secular movement and often saw religious groups as unsavory competitors. The Muslim Brotherhood, for example, initially supported Nasser but later opposed him because it became clear that he had no intention of establishing an Islamic government. Nasser attacked the Brotherhood with force and suppressed it after there were attempts to assassinate him. As Esposito points out, thousands of members of the Brotherhood were sent to prison, and several leaders were put to death.

The defeat of Egypt and other Arab states by Israel in 1967 left Pan-Arabism weak and discredited, and a generation of younger, more radical Arabs calling themselves Palestinians began to capture the imagination of the Arab world. The tension between the interests of existing governments and the program of the Palestinians was emphasized by the situation in Jordan. Nasser died in 1970, shortly after King Hussein used his military to attack the Palestinians in Jordan, an attack Nasser criticized but one he did not actively oppose. The unification of the Arab people was left at the time of his death an unrealized dream. John Esposito characterizes Arab nationalism as "idealistic, revolutionary, and ambitious." It affirmed, in his words, "an ideal rather than a reality."[23] Islam would ultimately replace Arab nationalism as a significant force.

ISLAMIC REVIVALISM

Groups such as the Muslim Brotherhood offered an alternative to the more secular nationalism of the Baath Party and Nasser. Hassan al-Banna, a schoolteacher, established the Muslim Brotherhood in Egypt in 1928. His ideas and his death at the hands of the Egyptian secret police serving King Farouk served to inspire followers. He did not simply turn to an Islam of the past, but rather attempted to apply "Islamic sources and beliefs, reinterpreting them to address modern realities."[24] In this respect, he attempted to distinguish his approach from the older Islamic modernism, which he believed compromised too much with Western ideas. Abul Ala Mawdudi points out that Islamic modernists were too quick to justify Islam by showing that it was compatible with Western thought:

> All these people in their misinformed and misguided zeal to serve what they hold to be the cause of Islam, are always at great pains to prove that Islam contains within itself the elements of all types of contemporary social and political thought and action . . . [T]his attitude emerges from an inferiority complex, from the belief that we as Muslims can earn no honour or respect unless we are able to show our religion resembles modern creeds and is in agreement with most of the contemporary ideologies.[25]

Islamic revivalism attempts to present Islam as entirely whole and self-sufficient, capable of providing an independent and complete guide for life in the modern world.

Hassan al-Banna argued that imperialism is a symbol of the West and a major threat not only to the political and economic life of the Middle East, but to its cultural life as well. The West is inherently corrupt and would eventually lead to its downfall. The secularism and materialism of the West contributes to injustice and oppression, but a hostility to imperialism was not equated with a hostility to modernity. His reflections on Islam were designed to provide an interpretation for a thoroughly modern way of life. He "addressed the problems of modernity, analyzing the relationship of Islam to nationalism, democracy, capitalism, Marxism, modern banking, education, law, women and work, Zionism, and international relations."[26]

Hassan al-Banna was critical of the West and reluctant to allow the West to provide a standard for the future, but he made it clear that the problems of Muslims were primarily caused by Muslims themselves. Esposito says that "rebuilding the community and redressing the balance of power between Islam and the West must begin with a call or invitation (*dawa*) to all Muslims to return to and reappropriate their faith in its fullness—to be born again in the straight path of God."[27] A social revolution was needed to invite Muslims to return to their faith. The leader of Jamaat-i-Islami in India, Mawlana Abul Ala Mawdudi, expresses the spirit of this project well:

> We aspire for Islamic renaissance on the basis of the Quran. To us the Quranic spirit and Islamic tenets are immutable; but the application of this spirit in the realm of practical life must always vary with the change of conditions and increase of knowledge. . . . [28]

New problems require new interpretations and the application of new technologies, but the principles are themselves immutable. The crucial role of Islam in this process of renewal means that Western democracy cannot be the model for politics. Both al-Banna and Mawdudi argued that simple majority rule led in the West to alcohol abuse and sexual laxity. However, participation of the people in terms of consultative assemblies that understand themselves to be subordinated to *sharia* are entirely acceptable. Western democracy is corrupt because it separates politics from the divine. Mawdudi did not see submission to Islamic law as a threat to true liberty, but his ideas of what might be called theodemocracy would not permit liberty in the sense that it is understood in the West.[29]

The Muslim Brotherhood suffered in Egypt under Nasser, and people like Sayyid Qutb encouraged a more radical application of Islam to the political problems they encountered. Qutb was a prolific author who believed that Islam offered a complete and distinctive social teaching. "Islam," he argued in his book *Social Justice in Islam,* "looks at man as forming a unity whose spiritual desires cannot be separated from his bodily appetites, and whose moral needs cannot be divorced from his material needs. It looks at the world and at life with this all-embracing view which permits of no separation or division."[30] The world as Qutb understands it is divided into two camps, the party of God and the party of Satan, and his imprisonment and torture in Egypt in 1954 after an attempt (to which Qutb was linked) was made to assassinate Nasser served to make his perspective even more revolutionary. Governments calling themselves Muslim were not sufficiently focused on the core principles of the religion. Only *jihad* (struggle) against the corruption of the West and the misunderstandings of existing Muslim governments could make a new Islamic order possible.[31] Muslims who failed to heed the call for the new order were understood by Qutb as enemies of God. Qutb became an inspiration to a number of Islamic groups after he was arrested again and executed in Egypt in 1965 by Nasser's forces.

The power of the Muslim Brotherhood was enhanced by Anwar Sadat, who seemed to favor a religious rebirth in Egypt. Although it was not recognized as a legitimate political party, it was allowed to meet openly and it attempted to work more peacefully within Egyptian society, finally losing Sadat's favor when it condemned the Camp David accords. The Brotherhood became important again in the 1980s as a social, political, and economic power. It sponsored banks, schools, and hospitals, and worked with the Wafd party to affect elections. A host of more radical Islamic groups were made possible by the pioneering efforts of the Brotherhood.

Selected Bibliography

Esposito, John, *The Islamic Threat: Myth or Reality* (New York: Oxford University Press, 1992).

Khalidi, Rashid, Anderson, Lisa, Muslih, Muhammad, and Simon, Reeva, *The Origins of Arab Nationalism* (New York: Columbia University Press, 1991).

Nasser, Gamal, *The Philosophy of the Revolution* (Buffalo, N.Y.: Economica Books, 1959).

Endnotes

1. Rashid Khalidi, Lisa Anderson, Muhammad Muslih, and Reeva Simon, *The Origins of Arab Nationalism* (New York: Columbia University Press, 1991), vii.
2. See Khalidi's "proposed revision of the revisionist theory" of Dawn in Khalidi, 52.
3. Khalidi, 9.
4. Bogle, 259.
5. "Ironic Origins: Arab Nationalism in the Hijaz, 1882–1914," by William Ochsenwald, in Khalidi, 189. My treatment of the Arab revolt draws heavily on this excellent work.
6. Ochsenwald, 191.

7. Ochsenwald, 193.

8. Ochsenwald, 196.

9. Ochsenwald, 201.

10. "The Hashemites," by Mary C. Wilson, in *The Origins of Arab Nationalism,* 212.

11. Wilson, 212.

12. Wilson, 214.

13. Bogle, 264.

14. "An Iraqi Ottoman Army Officer," by Reeva S. Simon, in *The Origins of Arab Nationalism,* 158.

15. Bogle, 265.

16. Deborah Gerner, *Understanding the Contemporary Middle East* (Boulder, Colo.: Lynne Rienner, 2000), 104.

17. William Cleveland, *A History of the Modern Middle East* (Boulder, Colo.: Westview Press, 2000), 397.

18. "Nasser and Neguib," by John Gunther in *The Philosophy of the Revolution* by Nasser (Buffalo, N.Y.: Economica Books, 1959), 81

19. Nasser, 34.

20. Nasser, 70.

21. Malcolm H. Kerr, *The Arab Cold War: Gamal 'Abd al-Nasir and His Rivals 1958–1970* (New York: Oxford University Press, 1971), 6.

22. Kerr, 29.

23. John Esposito, *The Islamic Threat: Myth or Reality* (New York: Oxford University Press, 1992), 72.

24. Esposito, 121.

25. "Political Theory of Islam," by Abul Ala Mawdudi, in Donohue and Esposito, eds., *Islam in Transition,* 52.

26. Esposito, 123.

27. Esposito, 124.

28. Esposito, 126.

29. Esposito, 126.

30. Esposito, 127.

31. Esposito, 128–129.

Chapter 6

The Challenge of Jewish Nationalism

The Jews' desire to establish a country for themselves in the Middle East has had a significant impact on the region. Tensions produced by the establishment of the state of Israel have affected peoples and governments. Today, almost every issue in the Middle East is in one way or another seen as related to the controversies surrounding Israel's existence, its borders, or its treatment of the Palestinians, and the constant threat of war has had an effect on the economies of every country in the area. Jewish nationalism, or Zionism, is understood very differently by its advocates than by its critics. Not all Jews would refer to themselves as Zionists, but most would accept the notion that there is a special connection between the Jewish people and the land of Israel, and most would argue that the Jews had a right to establish the modern state of Israel. On the other hand, the critics of Zionism see the movement as a manifestation of European imperialism and therefore argue that Israel's establishment was in some crucial respects illegitimate. The purpose of this chapter is not to settle the dispute or reveal that one view is right and the other view is wrong; rather, it is to lay out the differences so the depth of the disagreement can be understood.

There are two major manifestations of Zionism, and modern or political Zionism cannot be understood fully without an appreciation of its roots in premodern or religious Zionism. Even though many political Zionists were secular Jews, religious Zionism provided a crucial foundation for many of the political arguments supporting nationalism. Religious Zionism takes its bearings from the historical reality of an ancient Jewish commonwealth and its destruction by the Romans. The vast majority of the Jews were driven forcibly from the land of Israel by the Romans in the year 70 C.E. Approximately 600,000 Jews were slaughtered, some 300,000 were taken as slaves, and the Temple in Jerusalem was destroyed. After a second Jewish revolt was crushed in 135, the Romans renamed the land Palestine, meaning the land of the Philistines, to eliminate any sign of a Jewish presence. The dispersal of the Jews became known as the diaspora, and Jews from that time on hoped to return to their land. This emotional link with the land was embedded in the religious thought and ceremony of the Jews. Israel figured prominently in prayers, literature, and liturgy. The cycle of religious holidays was celebrated by Jews around the world according to the time of year in what had been Israel. For example, the holiday known as Sukkot celebrates the time of the harvest in Israel, not the time of the harvest in Europe or America. On the ninth day of the Hebrew month of Av, Jews fast and mourn the destruction of the Temple and pray for its rebuilding. Most famously, the Passover service ends with an emotional expression of religious Zionism: "Next Year in Jerusalem." Synagogues around the world are built facing east, so that Jews can pray toward Jerusalem.

Messianic Judaism holds that the coming of the Messiah will coincide with a return of the Jews to their land. Traditionally, religious Jews believed that the Messiah would himself be responsible for gathering the Jews once again in Israel, and some messianic Jews in Israel today do not consider the state of Israel legitimate because the Messiah has not yet come. Other messianic Jews believe that Jews should begin returning to what they consider to be their land as a precondition for the coming of the Messiah, that redemption will result from a return to the land and that this redemption will signal the coming of the Messiah.

The second manifestation of Zionism is political Zionism or Jewish nationalism. It is a specifically modern phenomenon, but it draws heavily on the foundation of religious Zionism. Political Zionism is a response to anti-Jewish activities in lands where Jews found themselves as a result of the diaspora. Some of the harshest persecution of the Jews took place in Russia, where since 1791 Jews had been confined to live in poverty in one region of the country, known as the Pale of Settlement. In the 1870s study groups began to form in Russia. These groups were known as Chovevei Zion, or Lovers of Zion. Classes in the Hebrew language and Jewish history were offered in secret and the hope of a return to Israel was kept alive.

After the assassination of Czar Alexander II in 1881, the Russian government sponsored massacres of Jews throughout the Pale. These attacks, known as pogroms, increased in 1882 under Alexander III, and hundreds of thousands of Jews were driven out of their homes. The Russian secret police, the Okhrana, also disseminated a now-infamous forgery called *The Protocols of the Elders of Zion*, a book supposedly written by Jews, outlining their plans for secret plots to take over the world.[1] This work was translated into every major language and has inspired hatred and persecution since it was published. By 1900, approximately 1 million Jews left Russia for the United States, and some returned to what had been Israel and was now called Palestine. Those who went to Palestine often had only a romantic view of Israel long past; they felt an emotional link with Israel as it once existed, and they believed that they could make a better life for themselves there. Clearly, the land had come under new ownership since the ancient kingdom, but Jews were optimistic about their future in Palestine and believed that the details of living arrangements could be worked out.

The persecutions in Russia inspired Leo Pinsker from Odessa to write his book *Autoemancipation* in 1882. His argument was that normal relations among people must be founded on respect, but human nature is such that a people like the Jews would always be regarded with suspicion. Since Jews had no national homeland, they would always be despised. Judeophobia, as he called it, was the natural result of the Jews' homelessness. Pinsker doubted that Jews would ever be accepted as full members of any non-Jewish country; they needed a national home. What mattered to Pinsker was the fact of a homeland. He did not in his initial formulation of the problem ascribe any special significance to the land of Israel. The Jewish homeland was not in his mind related to traditional religious longings or to any concept of the Messiah. It was a reasoned response to persecution. After Pinsker met with leaders of the Chovevei Zion at a conference he organized, he became convinced that only Palestine would work as a homeland.

The figure who transformed political Zionism into a strong, international movement was Theodor Herzl. He was comfortable for many years as an assimilated Jew from a wealthy family in Budapest. He received his law degree from the University of Vienna in 1884 and worked in the ministry of justice as he pursued his writing. At the age of 31, Herzl became the Paris correspondent for Austria's most important newspaper, and his coverage of the famous Dreyfus affair convinced him that hatred of Jews was not disappearing in the modern world, in spite of improvements in education and communication. Dreyfus, a Frenchman, was the only Jew on the French General Staff, and when evidence surfaced that someone on the staff was selling military secrets to the Germans, Dreyfus was charged. The true traitor was discovered very early in the investigation, but the military preferred to hold the Jew responsible. Dreyfus was court-marshaled and sentenced to life imprisonment. When a new chief of intelligence took office, he discovered the truth and brought the matter to public attention. Even after the true traitor had confessed to the crime, Dreyfus was found guilty in a second trial, although his sentence was reduced. Finally, in 1906, the new president of France ordered a review of the case and Dreyfus was cleared of all charges. What was especially shocking for Herzl was the anger that the French people felt toward Dreyfus. The image of mobs yelling "Death to the Jews" in what had seemed to Herzl to be a civilized and tolerant nation made a serious impression on him. The result was his famous work *The Jewish State*, published in 1896.

Herzl argued that hatred of Jews would not cease until Jews found a national homeland. He criticized the idea of a long-term, gradual exodus and recommended specific measures to begin a drive for a more focused nationalism. Two organizations would work together to create a homeland: one would handle legal

Herzl: The Jewish State

We have sincerely tried everywhere to merge with the national communities in which we live, seeking only to preserve the faith of our fathers. It is not permitted us. In vain are we loyal patriots, sometimes superloyal; in vain do we make the same sacrifices of life and property as our fellow citizens; in vain do we strive to enhance the fame of our native lands in the arts and sciences, or her wealth by trade and commerce. In our native lands where we have lived for centuries we are still decried as aliens, often by men whose ancestors had not yet come at a time when Jewish sighs had long been heard in the country. The majority decide who the 'alien' is; this, and all else in the relations between peoples, is a matter of power.

Arthur Hertzberg, *The Zionist Idea* (New York: Meridian Books, 1959), 209.

issues connected with the massive undertaking, and one would raise money for the project. Herzl began an active political career, visiting the sultan of the Ottoman Empire to try to arrange an agreement with him to allow the Jews to return to Palestine. He approached wealthy Jews for contributions, and he organized what became the powerful Zionist Congress, which met for the first time in Basel, Switzerland, in 1897. This organization set the goals for political Zionism: to establish a homeland for the Jews in Palestine in a way that would be accepted by public law. The focus on a legally recognized homeland led Zionist leaders to work with European countries, which seemed at the time to have world-leadership responsibilities, and with the Ottoman government. It is not clear that anyone really represented those who lived in Palestine. Herzl was convinced that Palestine was the proper homeland for the Jews, but he and others did consider alternative possibilities, including land in Uganda, which Herzl made clear would only be accepted as a temporary measure until a return to Palestine became possible. Herzl failed to realize his dream of a state for Jews in his lifetime, but when he died in 1904, he had succeeded in laying a foundation for such a state.

JEWISH IMMIGRATION TO PALESTINE

It is difficult to outline a history of Jewish immigration to Palestine without becoming embroiled in political disputes. Figures differ, depending on the source one cites and the political agenda of the historian. Beyond history, one has to take into account the issue of perceptions and beliefs, which may or may not be based on fact. Most agree that serious Jewish immigration began in the 1880s with Chovevei Zion, who established small, agricultural communities in Palestine. Once Herzl's influence was felt and the Jewish National Fund came into existence, a new wave of sponsored immigrants arrived, many of whom were socialists from Russia. They established new communities known as *kibbutzim*, where work was shared and property held in common. The pace of immigration increased rapidly. In response to repression in eastern Europe, Jews from Poland also began to make the journey, and after the rise of Hitler, Jews throughout Europe went to Palestine, dramatically increasing the Jewish population.

Palestine had been a depressed and neglected area under Ottoman rule, but changes in the economic conditions in the area also had an impact on Arab demographics. Scholars disagree about what is sometimes referred to as the issue of Arab immigration. Zionists argue that western Palestine (the part of Palestine now defined as Israel) was transformed by Jewish efforts from a desolate and unattractive area into a viable economic region and that new economic opportunities were created for both Jews and Arabs as a result. These improved economic conditions encouraged, according to Zionists, the movement of some Arabs from eastern Palestine (the part of Palestine now called Jordan) and some from surrounding countries into western Palestine. Some historians argue that Zionists exaggerate the extent of Arab immigration in order to suggest that the part of Palestine now called Israel was not desirable to the Arabs until after the Jews were there. If the Zionist argument were true, then Zionist claims to the land would be

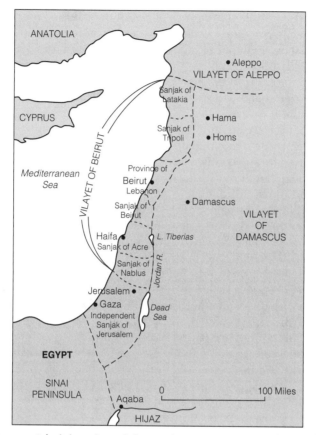

Figure 6 Ottoman Administration of the Region

strengthened. Scholarly dispute on this issue is hampered by the fact that poor (and disputed) population records were kept by the British between the two World Wars. However, it seems clear that some Arab immigration did take place at the same time that Jews were coming to Palestine in substantial numbers.

In order to accommodate Jewish immigration, Zionist organizations were involved in purchasing land legally, but these purchases were often from absentee Arab landowners. In other words, Jews who purchased land in Palestine did not deal with those who actually worked the land; the Arab peasants who actually lived on the land did not have the legal title to it under Ottoman rule. Zionists defend their purchases as proper, but the result was often the eviction of the poor Arab farmers by their wealthy Arab landlords. Problems also emerged as a result of the transition from the Ottoman taxation system to the British taxation system during the Mandate period. The Ottoman approach was to allow payment in the form of agricultural products. The British demanded payment in cash and many poor Arab farmers were forced to sell their land to wealthy Arabs or to Jews in order to settle tax debts to the British. The Jews who purchased the land were not responsible for the tax policies of the British, but they were one of its beneficiaries. Jewish land purchases were therefore made in the context of broader issues. The result of the purchases was increased tension between Arabs and Jews, or at least between poor Arabs and Jews. Violence began to break out, and the British were forced to keep the peace. In Palestine, ethnic, religious, social, and economic changes were taking place rapidly, and all under an uncertain political atmosphere.

Tensions between Arabs and Jews began to increase during the Mandate period, and the conflicts that emerged sometimes took on a religious tone, even though the reason for the conflicts may not have been religious. A good example of this was an incident at the Western Wall in Jerusalem in 1928. On the Jewish holiday of Yom Kippur, orthodox Jews set up a screen next to the Wall to separate the worship of men and women, as was their practice. Since the Wall is immediately adjacent to the al-Aqsa Mosque, any activity at the wall has an impact on Muslim Arabs. Some felt that the integrity of the mosque was threatened by the construction of the screen, and protests began. Jews felt that their right to worship was threatened, and Muslims held rallies to protect the mosque. In August of 1929, violence between armed groups broke out; after a series of attacks and counterattacks, over 100 Jews and over 80 Arabs were dead and almost 600 wounded. The British conducted an inquiry into the violence and concluded that both Jews and Arabs bore partial responsibility for the conflict.

Tensions between Jews and Arabs increased after Hitler came to power in 1933 in Germany and the persecution of Jews became more intense there, convincing many that it was necessary to seek refuge in Palestine. The difficult issue of immigration became even more volatile under these circumstances. In the United States, a convention of Zionists meeting at the Biltmore Hotel in New York in 1942 announced the Biltmore Program, calling for open immigration for Jews to Palestine and the establishment of a Jewish state. But Britain's perspective on Palestine was quite different. Still hoping to play Jews and Arabs against one another in the hope of advancing its own interests, Britain wanted to offer vague encouragement to Jews about immigration while holding to a strict immigration quota for Jews in order to calm the fears of the Arabs.

Jewish groups saw the immigration quota as disastrous and worked to bring Jews into Palestine, even if it meant doing so illegally. With limited resources at its disposal, the Jewish Agency procured ships that were often in poor shape to bring desperate Jews out of harm's way in Europe and on to Palestine. British authorities were often able to stop these ships; the passengers would be treated as illegal immigrants and sent to detention camps in Cyprus. Many ships still managed to slip past the British, and Jews continued to arrive in Palestine. Arabs resented the increase in Jewish immigration, and Jews resented the British attempts to prevent immigration. Jewish and Arab groups began to arm themselves, anticipating a general struggle.

By the end of World War II, the new United Nations knew it should address the problems in Palestine. It created the United Nations Special Committee on Palestine (UNSCOP) to study the problems there and offer recommendations. The report from the Committee suggested a second partition of Palestine (the area originally known as Palestine included the territory that was set aside in

1922 by Churchill for Transjordan). The new partition plan was not attractive to Jews or Arabs. Jews would receive slightly more than half of what remained of Palestine, but they would not get Jerusalem, which would be placed under international control, and the Jewish section would contain a large Arab population, which would make it difficult to imagine a stable country. The Arabs opposed partition because it legitimized a Jewish state in Palestine, which they saw as an extension of European imperialism. The Jewish Agency was disappointed with the partition plan, but accepted it. The Arab League made it clear that war would be the inevitable result of partition. In a dramatic session, the General Assembly of the United Nations voted to accept the partition plan with minor modifications on November 29, 1947. With fighting already breaking out, the British left Palestine in frustration on May 14, 1948, ending their mandate. By the end of the same afternoon, David Ben-Gurion proclaimed the state of Israel. The next day, armies from six Arab states (Syria, Transjordan, Egypt, Saudi Arabia, Lebanon, and Iraq) began military action against the new country.

THE REFUGEE PROBLEM

What happened during what the Israelis call the War of Independence and what Palestinians call *al-Nakba* ("the catastrophe") is of crucial importance for understanding and evaluating Zionism. The problem with studying what is often referred to as the first Arab-Israeli war is that almost every fact is in dispute, even the names used to identify the facts. So much depends on how these early events are seen and interpreted that one can barely report a single incident without seeming to side with one perspective or another. Perhaps the most important question of the war is what caused approximately 600,000 (the number is in dispute) Arabs to leave their homes in Palestine. The people who now call themselves Palestinians (the name was not current in 1948) see this as one of the main events that defines their current claim to land and to a Palestinian state.

The crucial disagreement is over whether the Arabs who left their homes fled on their own, or whether they were driven out by the Israelis. Perhaps it is better not to refer to this as a mere disagreement. Both sides consider the matter so closed that even raising the issue seems absurd or insulting to one side or the other. The class of beliefs must still be explored, and it makes sense to discuss these beliefs first in their pristine form, before analyzing recent scholarship that many believe has settled the dispute.

What has become known in recent years as the Palestinian position is that the Israelis used the war as an excuse to clear the land of what they believed to be an undesirable population. Attacks against the Arabs were part of the plan to create an Israel free of Palestinian complications. Some even suggest that the actions of the Israelis at the time constituted a kind of ethnic cleansing, a version of genocide against the Arab population. This claim (which is not made by all Palestinians) means that the Israelis were guilty of essentially the same kind of policy of extermination and relocation carried out earlier by the Nazis. According to this perspective, Israeli forces attacked Arab villages, slaughtered men, women, and children, and destroyed Arab homes. The Israeli government also encouraged nongovernmental groups such as the Irgun to attack Arab civilians as well; since these groups were not officially representing Israel, their actions could be publicly condemned but privately condoned.

Palestinians also claim that the Israelis broadcast frightening stories of terrible epidemics sweeping the countryside and warned Arabs that they would be killed if they remained. A well-respected journalist, Erskine Childres, wrote a now-famous critique of Israel's actions during the war. "It is clear beyond all doubt that official Zionist forces were responsible for expulsion of thousands upon thousands of Arabs, and for deliberate incitement to panic."[2]

Palestinians argue that they have sympathy for the plight of the Jews and an understanding that they have suffered persecution around the world, but they argue that the fact of that persecution does not justify the persecution of Palestinians. Jews may feel that they need a homeland, but they had no right to drive the Palestinians off their land in order to achieve their goals. This version of the events during the war serves as the foundation for recent demands by Palestinians for a right of return of refugees and their descendants to the land that they believe was wrongfully taken after they were driven away by force.

Zionists offer a completely different version of the facts. They claim that the official policy of the new Israeli government was to urge Arabs to stay and to reassure them that they were not targets of the Israeli military. Israelis say that urgent appeals were made over the radio for the Arabs to remain calm and not to leave. It was, according to the Zionist argument, in the interest of the Israelis to defend their new country, but it was not their desire to attack the Arab population. Israelis and their supporters say that Arabs were actually frightened by the invading Arab armies, which let it be known that any Arabs staying in Israel would be treated as collaborators and killed if found. In addition to this, atrocity stories were fabricated by Arab leaders to further their goal of creating mass Arab flight. This was supplemented by Arab assurances that the war would be won quickly and the Arab population could be confident of returning to its homes triumphantly. This perspective is offered by a former Israeli representative to the United Nations (later to become Israeli Foreign Minister), Abba Eban: "Caught up in the havoc and tension of war; demoralized by the flight of their leaders; urged on by irresponsible promises that they would return to inherit the spoils of Israel's destruction—hundreds of thousands of Arabs sought the shelter of Arab lands."[3] Eban supported his argument with reports from various international organizations and what he claimed were independent observers. This argument of his, of course, is rejected along with his evidence by a number of recent historians, including Israeli historians, as will be shown. Zionists and their supporters also claim that during the decade following the war, approximately 600,000 Jews were forced to leave their homes and property in the Arab states where they had lived for generations.

Israel absorbed the Jewish refugees and Zionists suggest that the Arab refugees of the war could have been easily absorbed into the surrounding countries, except that the suffering of the Arab refugees was needed for propaganda purposes by the Arab states in order to wage a war of public opinion against Israel. In other words, the Arab states refused to help fellow Arabs, preferring to advance their anti-Israel political agenda. This Zionist argument completely exonerates Israel from responsibility for Arab refugees. The Arabs made their choices and while one can sympathize with the suffering they have endured since 1948, that suffering is ultimately the result of the choices they made.

A third position, often referred to as post-Zionism, is offered by revisionist historians such as Simha Flapan and Benny Morris.[4] The goal of these historians has been to illustrate that the Zionist claims are essentially mythical. They acknowledge that stories exist about Arabs fleeing their homes in 1948, but they argue that the facts do not support the stories, that Israelis cannot avoid the harsh truth that their country was founded on a basic injustice. Benny Morris states that his research did not produce any credible evidence that the Arab Higher Committee of Palestine issued blanket instructions to the Arab population to leave its homes. He uncovers credible evidence that Israeli forces were involved in the forcible ejection of Arabs, at least after the war began. Even more importantly, Morris claims to have found evidence that an important committee, a "transfer committee," existed as early as 1937 to plan the expulsion of the Arabs. If historians like Morris are correct, then the moral superiority that Israel has always claimed over the Arabs cannot be maintained. It does not follow from Morris's thesis that Israel has no right to exist; rather, it means that Israel needs to negotiate with the Palestinians in an entirely different spirit. Taking into account its responsibility for the plight and for the suffering of the Palestinians should be the first step in any conversations about a Palestinian state.

ZIONISM ON TRIAL

Beginning in the 1970s, concern about the plight of the Palestinians had grown to the point that Yassir Arafat, the leader of what was then known as the Palestine Liberation Organization, was invited to the United Nations to present his concerns. He presented the argument that Zionism is an ideology that is imperialist, colonialist, and racist. It is, he said, profoundly reactionary and discriminatory, representing a mirror image of antisemitism that is allied to racial discrimination. In 1975, the General Assembly of the United Nations granted observer status to the PLO and passed a resolution equating Zionism with racism (U.N. Resolution 379). It was not until 1991, during peace negotiations between Israel and the Palestinians, that the United States was able to sponsor a drive to revoke the resolution.

The most important attack on Zionism has come not from politicians or political organizations, but from intellectuals such as Edward Said, who first published *The Question of Palestine* in 1977. He analyzes the issue of Zionism in a scholarly manner, calling each of its claims into question. His arguments have been influential because they transcend the emotional diatribes that are so common with sensitive, controversial issues. He argues that one must, of course, sympathize with the Jewish victims of the Holocaust, but he asserts that Zionism intentionally creates a new class of victims worthy of the same regard: the Palestinians. The Zionists had a tremendous advantage over the Palestinians: they had a plan. The Palestinians were not prepared to compete with the detailed planning of the Zionists. They opposed what they perceived to be a more general, colonialist policy.

Said makes a powerful argument that supplements the work of the revisionist historians. If the goal of Zionism was to alleviate the suffering of the Jews by creating an equally powerful suffering for another people, then Zionism is fundamentally

---

Said: The Question of Palestine

But the success of Zionism did not derive exclusively from its bold outlining of a future state, or from its ability to see the natives for the negligible quantities they were or might become. I think Zionism's effectiveness in making its way against Arab Palestinian resistance lay in its being a policy of detail, not simply a general colonial vision. Thus Palestine was not only the Promised Land, a concept as elusive and as abstract as any that one could encounter. It was a specific territory with specific characteristics, that was surveyed down to the last millimeter, settled on, planned for, built on, and so forth, in detail.

Edward Said, *The Question of Palestine* (New York: Vintage Books, 1992), 95.

---

unjust. The fact of Jewish victimhood does not justify creating new victims. Of course, the issue is not one of theoretical argument; it is one of fact. Zionists continue to deny the factual claims of people like Morris and Said. Zionists have their historians as well. One such historian, Arieh Avneri, offers a different perspective on the facts. He says that the means employed by the Zionist movement were anticolonial. The Jews who settled in Palestine, according to his research, bought much of their land, treated their Arab neighbors with respect, and held out the hand of peace when war broke out in 1948. Political Zionism was not responsible for displacing the Arab population of Palestine. The victimhood of the Palestinians was caused by the Palestinians themselves and the Arab governments who found their suffering useful. Zionist historians attack the credentials of the revisionist historians, and the revisionist historians attack the credentials of the Zionist historians.

Once again, the issues of the Middle East fail to present themselves in an easily accessible form. What is the truth about Zionism? It seems that one cannot discover the answer by resorting to feelings. No one can measure the suffering of the Jews or the Palestinians. The answer, if there is one, lies in the facts, and the facts themselves are difficult to discover in the heat of argument. One thing is clear, there is a strong commitment in the Middle East to both versions of history.

Selected Bibliography

Morris, Benny, *The Birth of the Palestinian Refugee Problem* (Cambridge, Mass.: Cambridge University Press, 1987).

Sachar, Howard, *A History of Israel* (New York: Knopf, 1979).

Endnotes

1. Stephen Eric Bronner, *A Rumor about the Jews: Reflections on Antisemitism and the Protocols of the Learned Elders of Zion* (New York: St. Martin's Press, 2000), 3.

2. Walter Laqueur, *The Israel-Arab Reader* (New York: Penguin Books, 1991), 149.

3. Walter Laqueur, *The Israel-Arab Reader* (New York: Penguin Books, 1991), 77.

4. See Simha Flapan, *The Birth of Israel* (New York: Pantheon Books. 1983) and Morris, Benny, *The Birth of the Palestinian Refugee Problem, 1947–1949* (Cambridge Mass.: Cambridge University Press. 1987.

Chapter 7

The Arab-Israeli Conflict and Its Transformation

A number of serious controversies lay at the foundation of the State of Israel. The initial problems created by European imperialism were exacerbated by Arab and Jewish nationalism, and long-standing religious differences contributed to new tensions and misunderstandings. Once again, the problems of the Middle East appear to be layered, one on top of the other. When the 1948 war was over, nothing was settled. Israel turned to the business of creating a viable political community, but the Arab world did not accept its existence. The history of the conflict that followed can be divided into three periods: (1) the Arab-Israeli Conflict, which lasted from 1948–1967; (2) the Transitional Years, which followed the Arab defeat in the 1967 war and continued until Egypt signed a peace agreement with Israel in 1979; and (3) the Israeli-Palestinian Conflict, which continues even today. This chapter cannot offer a comprehensive history of this conflict, but it can illuminate some major events that may encourage more detailed study.

THE ARAB-ISRAELI CONFLICT

The challenges to Israel's existence were initially framed in terms of opposition by Arab governments that saw themselves in one way or another as representing one people, one Arab nation. Even as this sense of solidarity began to evaporate, the existence of Israel as a common enemy helped Arab governments rally around a cause and cling to the notion that the imagined solidarity might be maintained. For approximately 20 years after Israel declared independence, the Arab world was essentially dominated by one figure: Gamal Abd al-Nasser, and the Arab-Israeli Conflict in its original form is in many ways a reflection of his priorities.[1] King Farouk of Egypt was overthrown in 1952, and by 1954, Nasser had assumed control of the revolution. All of this was taking place during the early stages of the competition between the Soviet Union and the United States. The U.S. policy of containment that characterized the Cold War had ramifications for the Middle East. After President Truman encouraged Greece and Turkey to become full members of NATO in 1952, the Baghdad Pact was negotiated in 1955.

It was an alliance that included Turkey, Iraq, Britain, Pakistan, and Iran designed to oppose what were perceived as Soviet expansionist aspirations. The United States was the moving force behind the alliance, and in many ways the Baghdad Pact signaled the replacement of Britain by the United States as the main Western actor in the Middle East.[2] Nasser used his influence to discourage Jordan and Syria from joining the Pact and turned to the Soviet Union for military assistance the same year (in the form of an exchange of Czechoslovakian arms for Egyptian cotton).

In a move designed to signal defiance of the West, Nasser recognized Communist China and accepted a large loan from the Soviet Union, prompting the United States to withdraw its promised financial support for the building of the Aswan Dam. Shortly thereafter, Nasser responded by nationalizing the Suez Canal and telling Americans, "Go choke on your fury."[3] At the same time, Nasser was encouraging guerrilla activity against Israel and proclaiming openly that he supported its destruction. On July 5, 1956, Nasser said, "The hour is approaching when [we] . . . will stand in the front ranks of the battle against imperialism and its Zionist ally." The president of Syria and close ally of Nasser, Shurki al-Quwatli, stated that "the present situation demands the mobilization of all Arab strength to liquidate the state that has arisen in our region."[4] Whether or not these statements reflected actual military goals, they were taken seriously in Israel. David Ben-Gurion, the prime minister of Israel, saw the attacks and the public threats as warning signs that Israel was in danger. In addition, since 1949 Egypt had forbidden Israeli ships to use the Suez Canal and had blocked the Strait of Tiran, closing off Israel's southern access to shipping from the Israeli port of Eilat.

The war that followed these events in 1956 was sponsored by France and Britain, who felt especially threatened by the nationalization of the Suez Canal. They approached Israel to plan a coordinated attack on Egypt. Operation Musketeer, as it was called, was a military success and a diplomatic disaster. President Eisenhower was furious with Israel, which had staged this attack without his knowledge immediately before U.S. elections. He was particularly concerned that this illegal action by our allies would make our opposition to the Soviet invasion of Hungary seem hypocritical. The Soviet Union, which was focusing on problems in Hungary at the time, also condemned the attack on Egypt, but it refused to offer any direct military assistance to Nasser. International pressure forced France, Britain, and Israel to withdraw their troops, and Nasser emerged from what was clearly a military defeat as an Arab hero. Israel also got what it wanted: access to shipping through the Strait of Tiran, which remained open for 11 years. After the war, tensions increased. In 1960, Nasser proclaimed before the U.N. that "the only solution to Palestine is that matters should return to the condition prevailing before the error was committed—i.e., the annulment of Israel's existence." In 1964, he followed up on this theme by saying that "there is no room for Israel within the Arab nation."[5] The Palestine Liberation Organization (PLO) met for the first time in 1964, and Nasser was instrumental in choosing its first leader, who was replaced in 1969 by Yassir Arafat. Israel continued to read Arab words and actions as a challenge to its existence, and Arabs continued to see Israel as nothing more than an extension of Western imperialism. In the meantime, the United States and the Soviet Union began to view the Middle East as an important battleground for the Cold War, and each sent financial support and military equipment into the area, ensuring that any future conflict would be more serious than those in the past.

In May of 1967, tensions increased between Israel and Syria, each accusing the other of attacks. A number of skirmishes took place between Israeli and Syrian troops, each side claiming that its military operations were in retaliation for the actions of the other. Nasser hoped to strengthen his image as a protector of the Arab world by sending troops into the Sinai, supported by new commitments of cooperation with Jordan and Iraq. He also demanded that the U.N. Emergency Force (UNEF) stationed in the Sinai after 1956 as a buffer between Egypt and Israel be evacuated. In a defiant move, Nasser announced on May 21 that he was once again establishing a blockade of the Strait of Tiran, the very move that figured so prominently in the 1956 conflict.

War began on June 5, 1967, and was over in six days. The Israelis took over the entire Sinai Peninsula, the Gaza Strip, the West Bank of the Jordan (including East Jerusalem), and the Golan Heights. From the perspective of the Israelis, the war had been defensive and enemy territory had been taken only because they were forced to resort to military action in a fight for survival. It is important to recognize that Israel did, in fact, initiate full-scale military action. From Nasser's perspective, Israel's existence was itself an act of war and the Arab world was only defending itself. The problem, in his view, was not Egyptian aggression; Israel had stolen Arab land and this injustice had to be challenged.

The dynamics of the Arab-Israeli Conflict changed dramatically after the 1967 war. The defeat of the combined armies of Egypt and her allies was an embarrassment to Arab governments, and served as an invitation to new, unconventional groups like the PLO to take over the struggle against Israel. The new territory under Israel's control had an Arab population of approximately 1 million. It eventually became clear to the Israelis that they had a choice to make: return all the land captured in the war or maintain control of a resentful and largely hostile population. One thing was clear: the world would no longer see Israel as a weak, suffering underdog in the Arab-Israeli Conflict. Israelis would now be seen as aggressive victors, not victims.

The U.N. attempted to establish a diplomatic foundation for peace through the Security Council's unanimous passage of what has become the famous Resolution 242. This resolution was acceptable to everyone on the Council partly because of its ambiguity, and the Arabs and Israelis have consequently read the resolution very differently. Resolution 242 begins by "emphasizing the inadmissibility of the acquisition of territory by war." While this statement follows the principles of the U.N. Charter, it clearly stands in opposition to historical precedent, since most wars have resulted in changes in boundaries, whether or not those changes are technically legal according to international standards. The resolution clearly states that Israel should not expect to hold onto any of the territory it took during the war. On the other hand, the resolution also states that every country in the area should be able to "live in security." This would seem to imply that Israel would not have to return land until it was convinced that security was

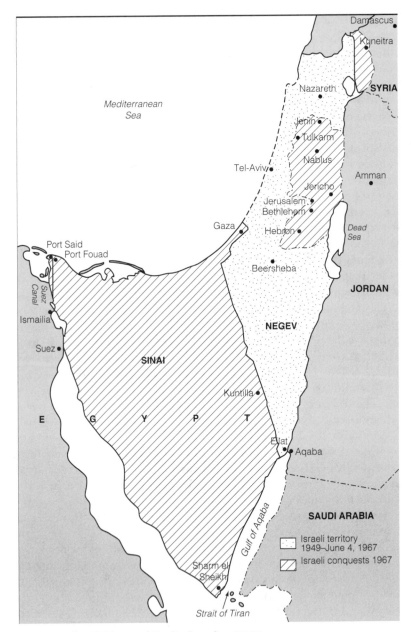

Figure 7.1 Israel and Disputed Territories after 1967

clearly guaranteed. The resolution also accepts as a matter of international law that Israel has the right to exist, something that Nasser and the PLO had been denying for some time. The resolution states that freedom of navigation should be allowed in international waterways, but Nasser had been denying that the Strait of Tiran was an international waterway; his argument was from the beginning that the Strait was part of Egyptian territory. The resolution did not solve any of the basic issues of the Arab-Israeli Conflict, but it did establish the principle of "land for peace," which would be the foundation of what later became known as the Peace Process.

THE TRANSITIONAL YEARS: 1967–1979

While Nasser was alive, he worked to bring the Arab people together, and although true Arab unity never existed, Pan-Arabism did not fade (at least as an aspiration) until his death in 1970. Sadat's assumption of power signaled a new era in the Middle East, a time of change and a turning to more limited ideas of nationhood. Sadat was interested in strengthening Egypt as an independent country; this change of attitude would eventually lead to the signing of an independent peace with Israel, but not before one more terrible war was fought. The Egyptian economy had been devastated by the constant conflict with Israel, but Sadat believed that an acceptable peace could not be achieved from the position of weakness. The 1973 War was almost certainly launched in an attempt to reestablish a more equal power relationship between Israel and Egypt, in order to provide a foundation for international involvement in peace negotiations on terms that Egypt could accept. Sadat's hope was to use war as an instrument of diplomacy, as one scholar puts it.[6]

The 1973 war was waged during two religious holidays, Ramadan and Yom Kippur.[7] Egypt hoped to gain an advantage in the conflict by sending troops into Israeli-controlled territory on the holiest day of the Jewish year, the Day of Atonement, when Jews everywhere fast for 24 hours and pray for forgiveness for the sins of the last year. Because of the holiday, Jews were focused on religious rather than military affairs; in fact, many regular troops were on leave and were temporarily replaced by reservists. Egypt sent troops across the Suez Canal and took over part of the Sinai, while Syrian troops attacked the Golan Heights. The war was more serious and more devastating than any of the previous wars, because the superpowers were determined to supply the Middle East with weapons to advance their own agendas. The Soviet Union sent an enormous number of weapons to Egypt and Syria, and the United States sent a comparable amount of arms to Israel. During the war, Israel lost 500 tanks, 120 aircraft, and about 2,400 lives. Egypt and Syria lost 1,100 tanks, 450 aircraft, and almost 8,000 lives.[8] But the Israelis were successful in defending themselves against their opponents again and drove into Syria, coming within 22 miles of Damascus. On the Egyptian front, the Israelis crossed over to the west bank of the Suez Canal and completely surrounded the Third Army. Only intervention by the United States kept the Third Army from being destroyed. From the perspective of Israel, its military victory was somber, not at all like the victory in 1967. It had driven the enemy back, but Israel had to face the fact that it was clearly more vulnerable than it had believed. The armies of Syria and Egypt fought well and inflicted serious damage on Israel.

Sadat's military initiative was successful enough to allow him to negotiate with Israel from a position of relative strength. Peace was important for him because it seemed to be the only way for Egypt to address its serious economic problems. Sadat introduced economic reforms shortly after the war, but they were not resulting in any significant improvements. In 1977 when he announced reductions of food subsidies, antigovernment riots broke out in Cairo and the army had to fire on civilians before order could be restored.[9] The year was one of changes. In Israel, the conservative Likud Party came to power, indicating that the people were dissatisfied with the way the more liberal Labor Party had handled the 1973 war. Itzhak Rabin, who had followed Golda Meir as prime minister was replaced by Menachem Begin, who had been a leader of the Irgun. In the United States, Jimmy Carter came to office, anxious to address Middle East issues. Sadat announced in a speech to the Egyptian National Assembly that he was willing to go to Israel if necessary to pursue peace. Begin responded by issuing a formal invitation to any Arab leader to come to Jerusalem. Sadat surprised the world by accepting the offer and going to Israel in November of 1977. Sadat's move had in some ways set aside all the efforts that President Carter had been making to work toward a peace conference in Geneva, but Carter recovered and took advantage of the moment by inviting Sadat and Begin to come to Camp David to work on a peace agreement. Carter was convinced of what turned out to be correct, that Sadat was more interested in making peace with Israel than he was in settling the issue of the Palestinians.[10]

The Camp David Accords consisted of two basic agreements, a Framework for Peace in the Middle East that called for negotiations involving Egypt, Israel, Jordan, and some unspecified representatives of the Palestinian people to address the issues of autonomy for the West Bank and the Gaza Strip after a transitional period of five years. But the second agreement, the Framework for the Conclusion of a Peace Treaty between Egypt and Israel, was more specific and led to the first peace treaty between Israel and an Arab state. Israel agreed to give up land for peace; it agreed to withdraw from the entire Sinai over a period of three years. Egypt agreed to allow Israeli ships to use to Suez Canal and to normalize economic relations. Sadat's decision to avoid linkage of peace to the Palestinian issue made the treaty possible, but it also led to strong criticisms from other Arab leaders. Egypt was voted out of the Arab League, and most Arab states withdrew diplomatic recognition of Egypt. In February of 1980, Egypt became the first Arab country to establish diplomatic relations with Israel. Opposition to Sadat had already been growing among those who were critical of his autocratic rule, and Islamic groups now began to condemn the peace treaty as an insult to the religion. Sadat was proclaimed a traitor to the religion and in October of 1981, he was assassinated by a fundamentalist group known as al-Jihad. Egypt had achieved an uneasy peace with Israel at great price.

THE ISRAELI-PALESTINIAN CONFLICT: 1979–PRESENT

With Arab unity shattered and the authority of Arab governments in question, the focus of the Arab-Israeli conflict changed. This was a process that cannot be assigned to a particular moment, but it is clear that sometime after the 1967 war, the plight of a what was coming to be seen as a distinct people, the Palestinian people, was seen as increasingly important. By 1979, the Palestinian issue was so important that Sadat's separate peace with Israel would be condemned for not dealing in a satisfactory way with it. By the mid-1980s, the Palestinian issue became identified as the central issue in the ongoing conflict with Israel. How this change took place is interesting in itself. Many would argue that the plight of the Palestinians was, from the beginning, the fundamental challenge to Israel and was simply not recognized as such by the leaders of the Arab governments or of Israel. Others counter with the suggestion that Arab governments simply decided to exploit the suffering of Arab refugees of the 1948 war, knowing that their suffering would be a public relations problem for Israel. Some have gone so far as to suggest that the term "Palestinian" was itself a propaganda tool in the struggle against Israel. This was, for example, the view of Golda Meir, former prime minister of Israel. In an infamous and widely condemned statement, she said that there was no such thing as a Palestinian people as a distinct group among Arabs. This view is not accepted by most scholars, but there is scholarly agreement that the term "Palestinian" was not commonly used to describe a distinct people until the mid-1980s. As Simona Sharoni and Mohammed Abu-Nimer point out:

> Only since the 1980s has the term Palestinian been integrated into the mainstream discourse on the conflict, and it has been used almost exclusively (including in Israel) in both scholarly and popular references to the conflict.[11]

The terms that people use to describe the issues of the Middle East are, of course, designed to promote the political perspectives of those who use them. When Israel came into existence, many Arabs refused to use the term "Israelis" to describe citizens of the new state because they denied the legitimacy of the state itself. Instead, the term "Zionist" was used, to imply that no real country existed but that Jewish imperialists were attempting to stake a claim on Arab land. Some continue to prefer the term Zionist to Israeli. The term Palestinian is also clearly controversial. If you use the term, you accept the idea that a distinct people with a claim to part or all of Israel exists. Some opponents of the Palestinian cause still refuse to say "Palestinian," preferring instead to refer to Arab refugees. But however the terminology is used, the fact is that the old Arab-Israeli conflict became the Israeli-Palestinian Conflict. This is a powerful example of the way in which language itself becomes embroiled in political controversy.

The theater of conflict moved from Egypt to Lebanon in the early 1980s, where the PLO had established itself to conduct operations against Israel. The government of Lebanon was extremely weak and did not know how to handle the presence of the PLO, whose attacks in Israel often prompted strong Israeli retaliation. Southern Lebanon became a war zone, with much of the Lebanese population in the area driven from its homes to avoid being caught in the middle of the cycle of attack and counterattack. In addition, long-standing tensions between Muslims and Christians were increasing; the political structure of Lebanon had never given fair representation to the Muslim majority, and new groups were challenging this in sometimes peaceful and sometimes violent ways. Christian groups who had traditionally controlled the government began to arm themselves and powerful militias emerged. Christians and Muslims (supported by the PLO) began to attack each other in what developed into a full-scale civil war, spreading throughout the country and eventually giving Syria an excuse to send troops into Lebanon.

Syria had for years claimed that portions of Lebanon were actually part of Syria, and this conflict provided an opportunity for Syria to strengthen its claim. By 1982, Lebanon was completely destabilized. As Cleveland describes:

> In the years from 1976 to 1982, the country disintegrated into a collection of sectarian enclaves, each defended by its own militia organization. Warfare between militia factions became a way of life, and the name Lebanon, which had once stood as a symbol for sectarian harmony, became synonymous with mindless violence.[12]

Israel had long-standing security concerns surrounding the presence of the PLO in Lebanon, and some within the Begin government thought the time was ripe to destroy the military power of the PLO in Lebanon completely by concluding a military alliance with Bashir Gemayel, the leader of the Phalangists, the largest of the Christian militias. Israel sent forces into Lebanon in June of 1982 with the stated objective of securing a 25-mile strip along the border in the name of safety, but troops under the command of Israeli Defense Minister Ariel Sharon advanced well beyond this point, even though the Israeli cabinet had never authorized a campaign this ambitious. With the help of the Phalangists, Israel's troops drove all the way to the capital city of Beirut and inflicted substantial damage to the military structure of the PLO, capturing 1,320 armored vehicles, 82 field artillery pieces, 62 rocket launchers, 215 mortars, 196 antiaircraft guns, 1,342 antitank weapons, and approximately 33,000 small arms. Unfortunately, the military tactic of heavy bombardment, which had been chosen in order to minimize Israeli casualties, resulted in a disturbing number of civilian casualties, even though the Israelis claim to have warned the civilian population by loudspeaker and leaflets in advance of the attacks (this claim is disputed). Over 6,000 were killed in the southern refugee camps alone. Christian forces in the area were unwilling to cooperate even with the Red Cross to allow treatment of the victims.[13]

In order to complete its assault on the PLO, Israel had to decide what to do about Beirut, where Arafat had secured approximately thousands of forces in civilian areas. The Israelis saw this as an attempt to use civilians as shields, but from the perspective of the PLO, it had no choice, since it was surrounded by the Israelis on one side and the Phalangists on the other. For the first time in Israeli history, a decision was made to begin large-scale bombing of an enemy capital. A number of attempts were made to target Arafat himself, who narrowly escaped with his life. Israel was prepared to continue its attacks until Arafat's force was neutralized, but the damage done to the city combined with the loss of life prompted the United States to work on a negotiated settlement. Eventually, an agreement was reached that traded Israeli withdrawal from the Beirut area for the evacuation of PLO forces to other Arab countries, including Syria, Jordan, and Tunisia. Approximately 15,000 PLO fighters were rescued and set out of the country.

World opinion had already turned against Israel. The war in Lebanon had been a television war, unlike any previous war in the Middle East, and the images projected to the world were painful. Reaction in Israel itself was similar to the reaction in America to its first television war, Vietnam. Scenes of destruction and misery were demoralizing, leading to public denunciations of the war by soldiers and a mass demonstration against the war in Tel Aviv of over 100,000 Israelis. There were calls for Sharon's resignation, and Jews in the United States were increasingly critical of Israel as well.

At this difficult time an event took place that in many ways came to define the entire war. Shortly after Lebanese President Gemayel was killed, Christian Phalangist troops entered two refugee camps called Sabra and Shatila and slaughtered somewhere between 1,000 and 2,000 men, women, and children. Many of the Phalangist troops who entered the camps were relatives of the Christians of the village of Damour who had been massacred by PLO forces five years earlier and had personal scores to settle. The Phalangists had been given clearance by Israeli troops to enter the area of the refugee camps, and Palestinians generally believe that the killings were either planned by or approved of by Israel. Critics of Israel openly compared Jews to Nazis, implying that an official policy of genocide was behind the attack. The entire world was stunned by the massacre, and Israelis themselves were horrified. Another mass demonstration—this time of approximately 400,000 people—took place in Tel Aviv. An official investigation of the Israeli government found that the Phalangist attack was not carried out with Israeli knowledge or consent, but that Israel should have been more prepared to anticipate the possibility of this kind of attack.[14] Ariel Sharon, who was the minister of defense then and the one who had planned the Lebanon invasion, was found by the investigation to be indirectly responsible for the massacres. Sharon was forced to resign from his position in the government, and many thought that his career was over. Those who believed that the Israeli government was engaged in a policy of killing were clearly not satisfied with the official investigation. Controversy continues to surround the incident and the investigation. Some sources claim that Israeli sentries in nearby high-rise buildings witnessed the massacres as they were taking place and that Israeli forces sent up flares at night to help the Phalangists with the killing, but these reports are denied by others. The truth will always be difficult to determine in situations such as this, when basic facts are disputed and there are substantial incentives for people on all sides of the issue to abandon any commitment to accuracy.

In the years that followed, there were a number of attempts to resolve the Israeli-Palestinian conflict. Jordan was particularly active in attempting to bring the parties to the negotiating table, but the PLO refused to recognize Israel's right to exist, and the Israelis refused to meet with the PLO, which it considered to be a terrorist organization. The PLO sponsored attacks against Israelis in an attempt to bring its cause to the attention of the world, and the Israelis focused on building new settlements in the West Bank and Gaza, hoping to settle the issue of ownership by creating a viable Israeli population in the disputed areas. This action was taken by the Israelis, even though international law forbids the transfer of a country's civilian population into areas seized by military force, and Israel was ordered to withdraw its settlements by U.N. Security Resolutions 446 and 465. Frustration among Palestinians in the West Bank and Gaza grew.

In December of 1987, an Israeli army vehicle lost control and ran into oncoming traffic, hitting a number of cars full of Palestinian workers who were returning from their jobs in Israel. Four people were killed and seven were badly injured, and rumors spread that the crash was intentional. As Thomas Friedman said about the incident, "Everyone knew that when it came to Jews and Palestinians, there were no accidents, only acts of war."[15] The funerals became political events and demonstrations against Israel spread quickly to the West Bank. This is the beginning of what came to be known as the *intifada,* or "shaking off." The Arabic word for revolt is *thawra,* and it is important to understand that this word was not used to describe the movement taking place. The Palestinians did not so much see themselves as revolting against the Israelis as striving to distinguish themselves from the Israelis. Unlike the terrorist activity of the PLO, the *intifada* represented spontaneous action of a frustrated population. In many ways, this was the turning point in the Israeli-Palestinian conflict, because world attention focused on the plight of the people who were protesting at a time when Israel's reputation was poor in the international community. As Sharoni and Abu-Nimer point out:

> Although in strategic terms the advantage still lay with the Israeli side, Palestinians had the moral high ground. For the first time in the history of the conflict, the David versus Goliath analogy was used in scholarly analyses and media reports, describing Israel as Goliath, the mighty aggressor, and the Palestinians as David, the underdog who is determined to win against all odds because his cause is just.[16]

The *intifada* consisted of a number of different forms of activity, from strikes to demonstrations, some of which became violent. But the *intifada* took on broad significance for the Palestinians. As Souad Dajani points out:

> The *intifada* started out as a struggle of an oppressed people to overthrow their oppressors. The dynamics of the situation were such that the *intifada* soon took on a momentum of its own and challenged the social and ideological underpinnings of the very people engaged in this resistance. The very act of resistance transformed the resisters.[17]

In other words, the Palestinian people in many ways developed a new consciousness as a result of their struggle. The battles that took place in the streets were one-sided; Palestinians did not have weapons at their disposal that could match the Israeli's weapons. The Israeli government saw the *intifada* as a serious challenge and responded to the violence in the streets strongly, hoping to bring the resistance to an end. Within a year, the conflict resulted in over 150 Palestinian deaths. The Israeli government defended itself, saying that it had a responsibility to restore order, but the number of deaths involved proved to some that Israel was devoted to a policy of destruction; at any rate, the deaths created a public relations nightmare for Israel, especially since many of the Palestinians who had been killed in the conflict were under 15 years old. Palestinians were unwilling to keep children out of the conflict, and Israelis were unwilling to allow the presence of children to weaken their resolve. The particular character of the uprising meant that violent confrontation would take place, and since the Israelis had a superior force, Palestinian deaths were inevitable.

The *intifada* was initially a spontaneous uprising (some have questioned this), but the PLO quickly saw its value and moved to take control. The position of the PLO was strengthened, in part, by a 1988 announcement by King Hussein of Jordan, in which he gave up all claims to the West Bank and recognized the

PLO as the sole legitimate representative of the Palestinian people. This, however, made the situation more complicated because the government of Israel still considered the PLO to be a terrorist organization and on principle refused to negotiate with it. By the time the energy of the movement dissipated in 1990, over a thousand Palestinians had been killed (although approximately 250 of these were killed by Palestinians who targeted people they considered to be collaborators). At this point, the attention of the world turned toward the complexities of the Gulf War.

Hostilities broke out again in 1996, when the Israeli government opened a new exit to an archeological tunnel in Jerusalem. The tunnel had been under construction for years, and the Israeli government had consulted Muslim authorities to ensure that all holy sites were being respected, but when the exit was opened, protests began and Palestinians went to the streets in defense of the Al-Aqsa Mosque, which some believed to be in jeopardy. As it was with the *intifada*, protests were violent, but more Palestinians had weapons now, and the Palestinian police who had been armed by the Israelis in accordance with the Oslo Accords saw itself as a protecting army and fired on the Israelis. The presence of weapons among the Palestinians prompted the Israelis to respond with increased force, and over 70 people were killed before the incident was over.

Israelis claimed that the incident a was not a spontaneous outburst of Palestinian rage; rather, they claimed, it was encouraged by Arafat to highlight new Palestinian concerns about Israeli claims to Jerusalem. As Chapter 10 will explain, the status of Jerusalem was not settled by the 1993 Oslo Accords, and by 1996, Palestinians were worried that Israel would succeed in convincing the world that there was no valid Palestinian claim to part of Jerusalem. The conflict over the tunnel in the name of the Al-Aqsa Mosque called the world's attention to Palestinian claims to Jerusalem. However, it is always difficult to determine with certitude whether events like these are spontaneous or planned, and claims and counterclaims will always be made.

Violence began again in September of 2000, when Ariel Sharon (the same Sharon who had planned the military action in Lebanon in 1982) visited the Temple Mount in Jerusalem and stated that he believed that Jews should always have sovereignty over what he saw as a Jewish holy site. Violence broke out almost immediately (some claim that violence had begun even before Sharon's visit), even though Sharon had cleared his visit with Palestinian security authorities the day before. The fact that he came to the Temple Mount with a large contingent of armed troops was seen as a provocation by many. Word spread that the Al-Aqsa Mosque was in danger and defensive measures were necessary. People took to the streets with rocks, as they had done during the *intifada*, but Palestinians had even more weapons now, and gun battles broke out for weeks, with rock-throwing children sometimes caught in the crossfire. Television images of well-armed Israeli soldiers firing into crowds of people, some with rocks and some with rifles, angered world opinion. Once again, Israel seemed to be responding to protesters with excessive violence. Hundreds of Palestinians were killed, and once again the presence of children in the violent clashes meant that a large number of children were killed by Israeli soldiers.

The United Nations condemned Israel, and a host of Arab governments spoke out strongly against what was often termed "Israeli genocide." Of course, Israelis were also killed, and a series of car bombs exploded in Israel during this time, killing a number of civilians. Palestinian snipers also committed a number of seemingly random murders of Israelis. Can a cause be isolated for this outbreak of violence? Clearly, the issue under the surface was the status of Jerusalem.

In July of the previous summer, a summit hosted by President Clinton at Camp David between Arafat and Israeli Prime Minister Ehud Barak had broken down. Perspectives differ on why the summit failed. President Clinton saw Arafat as responsible for the breakdown of the summit, since Barak had made what Clinton saw as significant concessions to the Palestinian Authority, including control over most of the West Bank and Gaza, authority over East Jerusalem and access to holy sites in the Old City. Arafat did not present a clear counterproposal at the summit, but he made it clear that the Palestinians wanted East Jerusalem as the capital of a sovereign Palestinian state; control over some territory and some Islamic holy sites under Israeli sovereignty was not sufficient. The atmosphere in Israel changed after the Camp David summit. Even though Barak had not offered everything that Arafat had hoped to gain from the meeting, it was from the perspective of the Israelis the most generous offer ever made by a head of state, and it seemed inconceivable that Arafat should not want to accept the offer. Even Israeli liberals, who had always stood behind the Peace Process, began to doubt Arafat's leadership. On the other hand, Israeli conservatives were shocked that any Israeli head of state would consider offering the Palestinians East Jerusalem, even if full sovereignty was not part of the deal. Meanwhile the Palestinians saw Barak's offer as another attempt by the Israelis to avoid the basic issues and block the creation of a Palestinian state.

It was in the context of these tensions that the controversial Likud leader, Ariel Sharon, decided to visit the Temple Mount (also the site of the Dome of the Rock and the al-Aqsa Mosque). His visit was designed to challenge the ruling Labor Party and the perception of Israeli conservatives that Prime Minister Barak was making too many concessions to the Palestinians during negotiations. Sharon wanted to highlight the concern of conservative Israelis who opposed any division of Jerusalem. Violence in the streets followed Sharon's visit, which the tensions that existed at the time made almost inevitable. The fighting continued and the movement that followed became known as the second, or al-Aqsa *intifada*. The Israelis were criticized widely for their use of force in opposition to the Palestinians. In October, the U.N. Security Council passed a resolution condemning Israel's use of what it considered to be excessive force.

But by the beginning of 2001, the situation in the Middle East had deteriorated significantly. Israelis and Palestinians seemed further apart than ever before. More martyrs were created and spectacular, mass funerals were being held for the victims of the violence. Prime Minister Barak alerted the Israeli military that it should be prepared for the possibility of regional war. The delicate peace that had been achieved with Egypt and Jordan was now in doubt as Arab governments proclaimed their support for the Palestinians. Arabs and Israelis were still at each other's throats, but the Palestinian cause had taken central stage.

The combination of a feeling of growing insecurity among Israelis and growing frustration among Palestinians helped to elevate Ariel Sharon to the position of prime minister in February of 2001. He won over Ehud Barak with 62.4 percent of the vote. Sharon was elected because a growing number of Israelis felt that their government had not been doing enough to ensure security for its citizens. Palestinians saw this election as a confirmation of their fear that Israel's talk about peace was insincere. One commentator on the election attempted to describe the reasons for this frustration, from a Palestinian perspective:

> There is undoubtedly no Israeli individual more universally hated or despised among Palestinians than Ariel Sharon. He masterminded and oversaw wars, invasions and massacres of Arab civilians. His resounding victory at the polls speaks more about Israel than thousands of deeply analytical works could ever do. Fifty-two years after the creation of a Jewish state in most of historic Palestine, Israelis have chosen a man with a violent racist past to lead them.[18]

Clearly, the Israelis who voted for Sharon would not accept this version of the facts, but it is important to understand just how significant the election was for the region. Sharon's public statements of general support for the Peace Process were greeted optimistically by the United States, but they were received with skepticism by Palestinians.

Sharon took the approach of responding to every terrorist attack against Israelis with a strong, military counterattack. The United States asked Sharon to reexamine his policy, arguing that the "cycle of violence" between Israelis and Palestinians was encouraged by retaliation on either side of the conflict. But after the September 11, 2001, terrorist attacks on the United States, President Bush began to express his dissatisfaction with what he saw as Arafat's reluctance to fight terrorism. In some ways, Bush may have been concerned that his effort to fight terrorism at home and in Afghanistan would be undermined by calls for moderation on the part of the Israelis. This new support from Washington encouraged Sharon to attack targets in the West Bank and Gaza and to openly threaten that if Arafat did not control terrorists, he would be removed from office. Some Israeli leaders, including former prime minister Benjamin Netanyahu (also of the Likud Party) hinted vaguely that Arafat himself might be targeted for assassination by the Israelis.

The conflict between Israel and the Palestinians has reached a new level of complexity and there is a very real possibility that a broader conflict is possible. The Israelis have lost interest in dealing with Arafat (see Chapter 10) and the Palestinians see Sharon as a destructive force. As Arafat attempts to deal with the demands of the Israelis and the Americans to fight terrorism, his authority has weakened among Palestinians. Groups like HAMAS and Islamic Jihad have strong popular appeal and offer the Palestinian people an alternative to Arafat. If a Palestinian state emerges from the conflict, it may be a very different one than the one envisioned by Arafat.

Selected Bibliography

Dajani, Souad, *Eyes Without Country: Searching for a Palestinian Strategy of Liberation* (Philadelphia: Temple University Press, 1995).

Quandt, William, *Camp David: Peacemaking and Politics* (Washington, D.C.: Brookings Institution, 1986).

Sachar, Howard, *A History of Israel* (New York: Alfred A. Knopf, 1979).

Endnotes

1. Howard Sachar, *A History of Israel* (New York: Alfred Knopf, 1979), 472.

2. William Cleveland, *A History of the Modern Middle East* (Boulder, Colo.: Westview Press, 2000), 269.

3. Howard Sachar, *A History of Israel* (New York: Alfred Knopf, 1979), 486.

4. Sachar, 488. King Hussein also communicated with Nasser, saying that "we look forward to the future when the Arab flag will fly over our great stolen country."

5. Sachar, 615.

6. Cleveland, 365.

7. Questions about war and religious holidays emerged again when President George W. Bush decided to continue his attacks on Afghanistan in November of 2001 during the holy month of Ramadan, in spite of protests from Muslims in America and around the world.

8. Fisher and Ochsenwald, *The Middle East: A History* (New York: McGraw Hill, 1997).

9. William Quandt, *Camp David: Peacemaking and Politics* (Washington, D.C.: Brookings Institution, 1986), 36. See also Cleveland, 368.

10. Quandt, 207.

11. "The Israeli-Palestinian Conflict," Simona Sharoni and Mohammed Abu-Nimer, in *Understanding the Contemporary Middle East* by Deborah J. Gerner (Boulder, Colo.: Rienner, 2000) 163.

12. Cleveland, 376.

13. Sachar, 182–83.

14. Sachar, 198. The Kahan Commission criticized Sharon, saying: "As a politician responsible for Israel's security affairs and as a minister who took an active part in the war in Lebanon, it was the duty of the defense minister to take into account all the reasonable considerations for and against having the Phalangists enter the camps, and not to disregard entirely the [possibility] . . . that the Phalangists were liable to commit atrocities."

15. Thomas Friedman, *From Beirut to Jerusalem* (New York: Anchor Books, 1989), 371.

16. Gerner, 179.

17. Souad Dajani, *Eyes Without Country* (Philadelphia: Temple University Press, 1995), 59.

18. Mariam Shahin, "The Coming of the Hawk," in *The Middle East*, March 2001, 4.

Chapter 8

Tradition and Modernization

The Middle East is a land of stark contrasts, and this is especially noticeable when one studies the movement toward modernization in the region. Ancient ruins stand side by side modern facilities. Traditional and modern dress mix in the marketplace. These contrasts reflect more than the fact of change; they indicate a real tension between cherished traditions and new ways. Questions emerge as modernization takes place. Is it necessarily a form of Westernization, and if this is the case, is it something to be avoided? Will modernization not only challenge traditions but destabilize countries by introducing new social, economic, and political dynamics? These issues stand at the center of a process of modernization that probably cannot successfully be denied or opposed.

In order to appreciate the significance modernization has for the Middle East, it is important to have at least a rudimentary understanding of what it is. Marion Levy has defined it as a relationship of human beings to technology. "The greater the ratio of inanimate to animate sources of power and the greater the multiplication of effort as the effect of application of tools, the greater the degree of modernization."[1] This definition, while helpful, seems to point to something more fundamental than the use of technology itself. Technology is an important factor in defining modernization because of the power it seems to give to one over his or her environment. As C.E. Black explains, modernization is "the process by which historically evolved institutions are adapted to the rapidly changing functions that reflect the unprecedented increase in man's knowledge, permitting control over his environment, that accompanied the scientific revolution."[2] In other words, modernization has as its premise the notion that human beings can increase their control over the natural and social world. Technology is one factor in this transformation, but as Bill and Hardgrave point out, modernization also involves organizational and attitudinal dimensions. In other words, as a country modernizes, it sees a movement toward specialization within society, and people begin to turn to reason rather than faith in order to address their problems. The specific form that modernization takes may be different from place to place, although it is often the case that modernization will involve a turn toward urbanization, a growth in literacy, the spread of mass communications, and a broadening of political participation. All these elements may accompany modernization, although they need not arrive as part of what might be called a "package deal."[3] In today's world, countries are more likely to be affected by other countries through economic and technological contact with them. This process of sharing between countries is known as globalization. The Internet is a new factor in globalization; its ultimate impact has yet to be understood.

There are clearly costs to modernization. "The process of modernization is disruptive, the source of discontent and social conflict."[4] But in the Middle East, there is great hope that modernization can take place in a way that is ultimately consistent with social traditions and religion. What is especially important to understand is that modernization does not happen quickly, and it does not take place in an orderly, linear manner.

C. E. Black argues that there are phases of modernization. First of all, a country must face *the challenge of modernity*, when traditions first encounter new ways and those representing the traditions must face challenges to their authority. Secondly, countries experience *the consolidation of modernizing leadership*. This phase can take several generations and involves the development of a new kind of political leader. The third phase is *economic and social transformation*, when changes move beyond the political sphere and society changes. This often means that societies that were once rural and agrarian become primarily urban and industrial. The fourth and last phase is *the integration of society*. Modernization tends to create the conditions for a fundamental change in society, one which goes beyond urbanization and industrialization. At some point, the structure of society itself is transformed.[5] These phases are not absolute requirements and do not take place in a mechanical fashion, but Black argues that an understanding of these phases can enhance our study of countries facing modernization. This chapter will examine creative tension between tradition and modernization by focusing on three countries: Iran, Jordan, and Kuwait.

THE CASE OF IRAN

In May of 1997, an amazing election took place in Iran, and Mohammad Khatami became president, beating right-wing candidate Ali-Akbar Nategh Nuri. The election was characterized by enthusiastic mass meetings that included women and children. A few months later, what Fariba Adelkhah refers to as a "carnival atmosphere" once again swept the country when Iran's soccer team qualified for the World Cup. When the players flew into Tehran by helicopter, crowds of supporters could barely be contained. These events were confusing to many in the West who assumed that Iran was a rigid, dismal religious society. Changes had been taking place in Iran since the revolution of 1979 that had gone unnoticed by many in the outside world. The image of the crazed, religious fundamentalist that Americans learned to fear that year has remained in the Western consciousness, but even during the years that Khomeini ruled, changes were taking place. Those changes were not defined by a struggle between two extremes. The issues for the country were not addressed by two opposite camps: the party of Islamic totalitarianism and the party of Western liberalization. Khomeini had already moved the country in the direction of a form of modernization, and Khatami did not see himself or portray himself as a challenger to the basic tenets of the Khomeini revolution.[6] The question for Iran has been, as Adelkhah points out, "how far Islam is able to invent a form of modern living that is compatible with democracy, capitalism, and the ordinary working of the international system."[7]

It may be helpful to see the changes in Iran as representing the *institutionalization* of the Islam of the revolution, rather than a turning away from the revolution. In other words, Iran is not secularizing or abandoning its grounding in religion, but the forms under which it follows religious principle are being regularized. The principles of the revolution are being integrated into the society as a whole. The role that taxes is coming to play in Iran can serve as an illustration of this point. There is a tension between the traditional animosity toward taxation and the need for funds to address social problems. Religious edicts had, for over a century, denied that the state has the authority to tax, as Adelkhah points out.

There are two principles in operation here. First of all, many consider it appropriate to claim tax exemption in return for acts of public generosity, such as making contributions for religious ceremonies, building schools, or sponsoring a sports hall.[8] Secondly, many hold to the idea embodied in Khomeini's *fatwa* ("ruling") calling on people to refuse taxes to an impious government. The current government has to address both of these attitudes. The government has to convince people that regular payment of taxes is needed and that widespread exemptions will make social progress impossible. The government also has to convince the people that it is sufficiently grounded in the principles of Islam to be worthy of receiving taxes. Article 51 of the 1979 Constitution addresses both of these concerns: "No form of tax will be enforced unless it conforms to the law. Conditions for tax exemption and reductions will be defined by law." Since then, religious leaders have offered significant support for the idea that an Islamic state can expect its citizens to pay taxes. Ayatollah Beheshti has proclaimed that "establishing an equitable taxation system to respond to the needs of the Islamic Republic's programmes is in perfect harmony with the principles of Islamic order."[9]

In 1989, Gholamhossein Karbaschi, the new mayor of Tehran began to work to beautify the city, which had grown to about 10 million inhabitants and was quite congested and neglected. One of his first projects was to encourage people to put pots of flowers on their front porches. This was very popular, but it was clearly not any kind of solution to the city's more fundamental problems, and his more ambitious projects required additional tax money. One of these projects is the establishment of small parks in the center of the city. These parks generally include benches, play areas for children, fountains, newsstands, and concessions for refreshments. The parks have had quite an impact on city life, because they allow a combination of traditional activities and new behavior. People can go to the parks to walk with their families or to pray, but the parks also encourage non-traditional activities:

> Most of these ways of making use of the open spaces involve new ways of living. Public parks are the principal places for practicing fashionable sports—aerobics and jogging in the early morning, table tennis and badminton in the afternoon—and eating pizzas, sandwiches and hamburgers . . . The parks are the setting for social innovation, though maybe at the expense of 'inventing tradition'; but they do not exclude old habits, which have even acquired some new legitimacy—people play chess and draughts there, they unroll their carpets and pray.[10]

Also, the parks now provide a place for young people to meet in nontraditional ways. Guardians of morality, known as the *basij* still exist and challenge those who seem to be acting improperly, but they can be avoided; they have been ordered to act in less coercive ways, and one can often be in the parks without seeing them at all.[11]

A tension still exists between the traditional animosity toward taxes and the need for urban renewal, which requires taxes. Karbaschi's initiative to build parks, however, does not represent a simple clash between religion and the secular sphere; rather, parks are presented as consistent with Islam, although new forms of contact and communication have developed as a result of the parks.

Another strong example of the phenomenon of modernization in Iran is what might be called the "bureaucratizing of Islam."[12] Religious education is becoming organized through schools and universities, rather than through sacred buildings. Admission to the schools is based on strict criteria, which include age and level of education, and it often involves regular examinations. Adelkhah points out that religious education is now more closely linked with national education, setting out career possibilities in the civil service. Since the 1990s, television plays a major role in religious ceremonies. The celebration of initiation into prayer (girls are initiated at 9 and boys at 15) is now frequently televised, suggesting a new connection between the public and private spheres of life.

The popularity of sports in Iran is also a sign of modernization. Soccer is the most popular, but volleyball, basketball, swimming, gymnastics, and even jogging have become important. Many of the larger cities organize soccer tournaments during the evenings of the month of Ramadan. It is true that Islam traditionally honors health and strength of the body, and sports are one way to achieve these goals, but contemporary sports are defined more by the thrill of competition, and this is something new. Institutions once known as Houses of Strength, where martial arts were practiced and important conversation took place, have been largely replaced by sports centers where people train for tournaments of various kinds. The emphasis on competitive sports also means that individuals must conform to

> well known written and standardised norms of modern sport, which are universal, public, and produced (or applied) by bureaucratic structures. The rules of football [soccer] are known to everyone, and are watched over not only by referees trained in specialized schools, but also by spectators at large, who are quick to approve or else shout abuse at referees' decisions during matches whose programmes are fixed by the Football Federation at the national level.[13]

The desire to compete has filtered into every part of Iranian life. People can enter contests to see whose sheep are the best, who are the best office workers, and who can paint the best poster promoting health. Contests are held to see who can recite portions of the Quran. In 1995, the *basij* announced that soldiers who could recite the Quran would receive extra leave, be allowed to pick their assignments, and be qualified for promotion. In April of 1997, 110 people who were able to recite justifications for the succession from the Prophet to Ali were given prizes of household appliances, carpets, and gold.[14] A weekly television show features a competition of the week, and the winner receives material prizes. More importantly, the spirit of competition suggests that some deserve to be honored for personal, particular skills that set them apart from others. This emphasis on the individual is transforming society, but the changes are not taking place in a spirit of challenge to the traditional life in Iran. In other words, the changes in Iran are not perceived by all to be a turning away from the principles of the Iranian revolution.

THE RISE OF REPRESENTATIVE POLITICS: JORDAN AND KUWAIT

Political development does not always accompany modernization. As Samuel Huntington said, "The primary problem of politics is the lag in the development of political institutions behind social and economic change." He points out that

> Political modernization involves the extension of political consciousness to new social groups and the mobilization of these groups into politics. Political development involves the creation of political institutions sufficiently adaptable, complex, autonomous, and coherent to absorb and order the participation of these new groups and to promote social and economic change in the society.[15]

Before the development of viable legislatures, other, more traditional systems existed in the Middle East that allowed for average people to bring their concerns to political elites. Informal assemblies known as the *majlis* provided opportunities for people to approach tribal leaders and solicit assistance. While these systems did provide channels of communication, they were limited in that the petitioner's power was defined by his power to make requests that could either be granted or not granted, according to the will of the leaders. The development of legislative bodies is important because it allows representatives of the people to limit or at least balance the power of elites.

Important political changes have been taking place in the Middle East since the 1980s. Legislatures have not, as a general rule, been important, independent institutions until fairly recently, but many in the West are unaware of the tradition of legislative politics in Arab nations. Reaching back to the very beginnings of Arab nations after World War I, legislatures have striven to be taken seriously, with different levels of success. Today, legislatures play a significant, if still limited, role in Arab political life.

JORDAN

It is fair to say that since the creation of Transjordan by the British in 1922 and its rise to independence in 1946, a struggle has taken place to institutionalize the role of the legislature.[16] The initial demands for the creation of a strong legislature were resisted by the British, who hoped to control the country through the act of installing Abdullah as king. By the late 1920s, the British decided it was in their interest to allow a legislature, as long as its power would be under the control of the king. The Legislative Assembly (or LA, as it was called) was elected in 1928, but it was so assertive that it was disbanded in 1931, after formally protesting its lack of real power. Abdullah continued to pursue a policy of limiting the powers of the legislature, while working to maintain the appearance of legislative involvement in politics. In 1951, the legislature embarrassed Abdullah by refusing to endorse his budget. This prompted Abdullah to dissolve the legislature again. Shortly thereafter, Abdullah was assassinated and his son Talal took over power. Talal supervised the creation of a new constitution, which has with a number of revisions remained essentially in effect to this day. The 1952 document made the cabinet responsible to the assembly for the first time. It also required that the prime minister and the cabinet receive votes of confidence before assuming power.[17] There are admirable general expressions of support in the Constitution for equality before the law (Article 6) and personal freedom (Article 7). Free exercise of religion is also protected, although there is a troubling exception to this; religious freedom is not protected if it is inconsistent with public order or morality (Article 13).

Since Islam is the state religion and Islamic law (*sharia*) is an important foundation for Jordan, conflicts between order, morality, and religion are bound to occur. The King retains power under the Constitution to declare war, conclude peace, and ratify treaties. This contrasts with the provisions for executive power in the U.S. Constitution, where the president is commander-in-chief, but Congress declares war. The American president may negotiate treaties, but the Senate must ratify them. The Jordanian King also has the power to wait six months after receiving legislation before returning it to the legislature with his signature (Article 93). If he does not sign legislation, the legislature may override his veto. In cases where there is a dispute, the courts can become involved, but judges are appointed and removed by royal decree. Once again, this contrasts significantly with the American system, where presidents nominate federal judges but the Senate has the power to reject them. Also, federal judges in the United States cannot be removed by the president. The most important power of the King is his authority to dissolve the legislature (Article 73).[18] Ultimately, a legislature can never be independent as long as its right to meet depends upon executive favor.

King Talal was asked to turn power over to his son Hussein, who became king in 1953. Within a few years, Hussein was faced with challenges to the concept of the monarchy, coup attempts, and Pan-Arabist denials of the existence of Jordan itself. He responded to these challenges by imposing martial law, banning all political parties, arresting political opponents, and closing down independent newspapers. For at least 20 years, Hussein managed the elections in Jordan to produce a weak legislature. However, it is important to note that even the legislature that was allowed to exist did accomplish some good. It was unable to challenge the power of the king in domestic or foreign affairs, but it did provide a forum for public discussion of civil liberties issues. This kept important issues alive in Jordanian politics.

From the mid-1950s through the late-1980s, the legislature continued to be an important presence in Jordan, even though political parties were banned throughout this period and the legislature was dissolved several times. It is important that whenever the legislature was disbanded, there were calls for it to be restored. As Baaklini, Denoeux, and Springborg point out:

> This suggests that years of parliamentary experience had a profound impact on the country's political culture, causing Jordanians to take it for granted that there should be an institution capable of overseeing the executive branch and providing popular input into the policymaking process.[19]

The legislature continued to struggle for independence through the 1990s. In 1993, for example, King Hussein succeeded in changing the election law in order to favor conservative families that supported the monarchy. Even this legislature refused to act in a docile fashion. It was initially referred to as the Yes Parliament, but it was an active, controversial legislature that raised questions about the 1994 peace agreement with Israel and the resulting economic ramifications for Jordan. On the last day of parliament's session in 1995, the Public Freedoms and Citizens' Rights Committee issued a report criticizing the government for making arbitrary arrests, banning public meetings, and punishing opponents of the peace with Israel with passport restrictions.[20] Although the legislature often opposed the king, the laws of Jordan allowed the king to simply bypass the legislature through the use of royal decree. For example, in 1997, the king issued a decree that imposed serious restrictions on the Jordanian press. It prohibited any news, views, or analysis that might "disparage the king or royal family, the armed forces, and heads of friendly states."[21] The decree also prohibited stories containing false information or rumors that would harm the general interest, government institutions, or government workers. These ill-defined prohibitions were a significant challenge to freedom in Jordan, and the legislature had no opportunity to debate them or vote on them.

Baaklini, Denoeux, and Springborg point out that despite a strong tradition of legislative aspirations and activity, "the Jordanian legislature can still function only within the constitutional and political space granted and tolerated by the king."[22] The lower house is elected, but the king appoints the members of the senate. This is significant because bills cannot become law unless they are approved by the senate. In addition, the king has an absolute veto over any bill and can suspend parliament whenever he wants if a veto is not deemed sufficient. Also, the parliament only meets for approximately five months a year, leaving the king to rule without legislative interference most of the time. Finally, the legislature is so poorly funded that it cannot study the bills that come before it or even research constituent inquiries. The meager staff that does exist is appointed by the king, so it has no loyalty to the legislature.

KUWAIT

The constitution of Kuwait was promulgated in 1962 by Abdullah Al-Salim Al-Subah, the emir of Kuwait, and defines the government as democratic. It calls for the protection of Islam as the religion of the state, the promotion of public health, science, letters, and the arts. Article 30 states that "personal liberty is guaranteed," and Article 34 announces that people shall be "presumed innocent until proven guilty in a legal trial." The right to private association and the protection of homes from illegal entry and search is also guaranteed. In spite of these strong endorsements, there are conflicting features of the constitution that call the country's stated commitment to democracy into question.

A strong legislature, the National Assembly (NA), is established, but Article 51 announces that legislative power is vested in the emir and the National Assembly together. This clearly violates the principle of separation of powers endorsed in Article 50, a principle essential to the independence of any legislature. The 1962 law defining elections restricted voting to male citizens over 21 years old whose families had lived in Kuwait at least since 1920.[23] This essentially limited suffrage to a conservative elite. The emir also appoints the cabinet, which is given the responsibility of controlling the departments of state (Article 123), and deliberations of the cabinet are secret. This gives the emir significant power over the everyday workings of the government. The real weakness of the legislature stems from the emir's power to declare martial law and dissolve the legislature. Martial law is proclaimed by decree, and does not require the approval of the legislature. Technically, the legislature must vote to support the decision of the emir within 15 days, but Article 69 states that if the legislature is not sitting, then approval of martial law will be the responsibility of the next legislature. These provisions giving the legislature some say in the emir's decision to proclaim martial law are qualified by the emir's power to dissolve the legislature completely. In fact, the National Assembly was dissolved in Kuwait from 1976 to 1981 and again from 1986 to 1992, a significant part of the entire history of Kuwait as an independent nation. During that time, the emir cracked down on the press, suspended sections of the constitution, and forbade public meetings of more than five people.[24]

It is also disturbing to note that the independence of the courts is compromised by the emir's powers. Article 164 states that the courts shall be regulated by law, but this is modified in times of martial law, when military courts take over and have the constitutional authority to hear cases in secret. The constitution was probably established partly to give a growing class of educated citizens the impression that their voices were important to the country. The emir also hoped to unify the country in the face of constant claims of Iraq to Kuwaiti territory. The emir hoped that the constitution would help to foster a feeling of allegiance to Kuwait as an independent country.[25]

The very fact that the constitution does provide for an elected legislature is important; from the beginnings of the country, the legislature has attempted to assert its power. As Baaklini, Denoeux, and Springborg have pointed out, "this assertiveness largely explains why Kuwait's parliamentary experience has been a tormented one."[26] Its aggressive character has led to its dissolution, but Kuwait's National Assembly has made a real contribution to public debate about the future of the country. The legislature has been the forum for what has essentially been a debate between representatives and an emir who is jealous of his power about how the country should be ruled. The National Assembly has been an especially important institution since the end of the Gulf War and its occupation by Iraq. New debates about economic and political reform have challenged the emir to look to the future in new ways.

Kuwait has a tradition of strong rule by the al-Sabah family, but even before the legislature existed, informal limitations on the power of the ruler did exist, especially stemming from the economic power of strong merchant families. One of the most important industries was pearl diving, and it provided a substantial income until the world turned to cultured pearls. Until the turn of the twentieth century, leading merchants were consulted when it was necessary to choose a new emir. In 1899, Kuwait decided to sign a treaty with the British that was designed to protect the country from the Ottoman Empire, but the country became what was essentially a British protectorate as a result of the treaty. The emir was emboldened by British support and began to distance himself from the merchant families that had been so important for the country's stability. After World War I, merchants responded to the new political climate by calling for the establishment of a *majlis*. Their recommendation was initially ignored, but a 12-member advisery council was established by the new emir after the death of Salim al-Sabah. Hopes were high that this would be an important change in the political life of the country, but the new emir never actually called a meeting of the council. Tensions between the emir and the merchants continued and in 1938, the emir was forced to agree to a document known as the Basic Law, which boldly established the principle of rule along with a National Legislative Council. The new council, however, was so aggressive, the emir responded with force. Most of the members of the council fled the country, but the head of the council was executed for treason.

The most important event preceding independence was the impact of new revenues from oil. In 1946, Kuwait received $760,000 from oil, but by 1953, that had increased to $169 million. These new revenues allowed the emir to shower his people with benefits and quiet the calls for reform. New jobs were created, and government-sponsored social programs were put into effect. Since the emir was no longer dependent on the economic power of the merchant elite, the political dynamics of the country changed. But interest among the young and educated in political change remained, an interest that culminated in the Constitution of 1962.[27]

The Gulf War introduced a new kind of dialogue in Kuwait. The emir found it increasingly difficult to oppose the calls for democratization after the United States led a coalition to protect it from Iraqi aggression. The Kuwaitis who stayed behind during the war had to feel that their efforts were appreciated, and the emir had to address those who criticized the Bush administration for risking American lives to liberate a country that was essentially autocratic. One reporter put it starkly when he said that Americans were being asked to make the world safe for feudalism.[28] This atmosphere of pressure to democratize led to an important conference in Jiddah, Saudi Arabia, in 1990. An agreement was reached there for the ruling family to receive support in return for a promise of reforms and the restoration of the parliament. When the war was over, elections were scheduled for October of 1992, and the period leading up to the election was dominated by far-reaching political debate, even though voting eligibility was still limited significantly. The emir attempted to return to the previously successful tactic of granting benefits to the population in order to secure their support. He wrote off most mortgage and consumer loans, provided $2,000 for everyone who had remained in Kuwait during the war, increased child allowances and support for widows, orphans, and the poor, and instituted a salary increase for every Kuwaiti employed by the government (which at that time was approximately 90 percent of the population).[29] The tactic did not work, and a number of opposition leaders (including radical Islamic leaders) were elected to the parliament. Elections were held again in 1996, and once again an independent, vocal group of representatives was chosen, although many of those elected in 1992 were unable to win reelection in the new parliament. And even though the power of the parliament was still limited, public debate had an impact on politics, especially on issues such as whether the labor code ought to be revised to deal in a new way with foreign workers in Kuwait.

The legislature in Kuwait remains constitutionally weak. The emir still retains the power to shut the government down and rule by edict. However, the political atmosphere in the country has changed and the voices of opposition to near-absolute rule have grown. The emir has lost his traditional allies and has moved reluctantly toward reform, but the domestic political situation seems to be tied to the international arena. Whenever a foreign threat has been on the horizon, the emir has tended to assert his authority over parliament and has been unsympathetic toward criticisms of the regime, especially when those criticisms have been rhetorically extreme and could be understood as a challenge to the country's unity.[30] The legislature has been an active and important part of Kuwaiti politics, but truly democratic institutions have yet to emerge.

The Middle East is changing, and social, economic, and political traditions are being either modified in ways that are consistent with what is perceived as the best in the tradition, or in more fundamental ways. Iran is attempting to find new ways to promote an Islamic life, while not rejecting the essence of the 1979 revolution. Jordan is working to strengthen the role of the legislature, and Kuwait is making its uneasy way into the future by balancing the security of rule by the emir with the untested voices of a divided people in the midst of a volatile international arena.

Selected Bibliography

Black, C.E., *The Dynamics of Modernization* (New York: Harper and Row, 1966).

Gaaklini, Abdo, Denoeux, Guilain, and Springborg, Robert, *Legislative Politics in the Arab World* (Boulder, Colo.: Rienner, 1999).

Zubaida, Sami, *Islam: The People and the State* (New York: I.B. Tauris, 1993).

Endnotes

1. James Bill and Robert Hardgrave, Jr., *Comparative Politics: The Quest for Theory* (Columbus: Charles Merrill, 1973), 63.

2. Bill and Hardgrave, 63. See also C.E. Black, *The Dynamics of Modernization* (New York: Harper and Row, 1966), 7.

3. Bill and Hardgrave, 63.

4. Bill and Hardgrave, 64.

5. C.E. Black, *The Dynamics of Modernization* (New York: Harper and Row, 1966), 66–67. This theory is discussed in Bill and Hardgrave, 65.

6. See Sami Zubaida, *Islam: The People and the State* (New York: I.B. Tauris, 1993), 13. Zubaida argues that Khomeini's political doctrines themselves are innovations and while respectful of Islam represent fundamental transformations.

7. Adelkhah, 2.

8. Adelkhah, 10.

9. Adelkhah, 12. See also page 114, where the relationship between *khoms* (one-fifth of income) and *zakat* (which only applies to certain kinds of income), is discussed.

10. Adelkhah, 19.

11. "Iran: Testing the Waters of Reform," by Fen Montaigne in *National Geographic*, vol. 196, no.1, July 1999, 2–33.

12. Adelkhah, 113.

13. Adelkhah, 144.

14. Adelkhah, 147.

15. Samuel Huntington, *Political Order in Changing Societies* (New Haven, Conn.: Yale University Press, 1968), 5 and 266. These passages are quoted in James Bill and Robert Hardgrave, *Comparative Politics* (Columbus: Charles Merrill, 1973), 77.

16. Abdo Baaklini, Guilain Denoeux, and Robert Springborg, *Legislative Politics in the Arab World* (Boulder, Colo.: Rienner, 1999). My discussion of Arab legislatures draws heavily from this excellent study. See especially Chapters 7 and 8.

17. Baaklini, Denoeux, Springborg, 139.

18. The legislature will automatically reconvene after a period of time, unless the king does not think conditions are favorable to a new election.

19. Baaklini, Denoeux, and Springborg, 145.

20. Baaklini, Denoeux, and Springborg, 162.

21. Baaklini, Denoeux, and Springborg, 163.

22. Baaklini, Denoeux, and Springborg, 165.

23. Baaklini, Denoeux, and Springborg, 176.

24. Baaklini, Denoeux, and Springborg, 184.

25. Baaklini, Denoeux, and Springborg, 177.

26. Baaklini, Denoeux, and Springborg, 169. My discussion of Kuwait's legislative history is greatly indebted to this analysis.

27. Baaklini, Denoeux, and Springborg, 175.

28. Baaklini, Denoeux, and Springborg, 187.

29. Baaklini, Denoeux, and Springborg, 190.

30. Baaklini, Denoeux, and Springborg, 197.

Chapter 9

The Confrontation With Terror

On September 11, 2001, terrorists struck the United States, killing 2,823 men, women, and children, including rescue workers and police who died attempting to help the victims. Two hijacked airplanes along with their civilian passengers and crew were flown directly into the twin towers of the World Trade Center in New York, causing them both to collapse. A third was flown with its civilian passengers and crew into the Pentagon in Washington, D.C., and a fourth hijacked plane with its passengers and crew crashed in Pennsylvania, presumably before the plane could reach its intended target, and after a struggle on board between passengers and terrorists. As federal investigators began to gather information about the attack, suspicion was quickly centered on the infamous Osama bin Laden, a terrorist who had for many years been organizing and training his terrorist organization in Afghanistan. Until this attack, the average American had watched the Middle East with uneasy interest, believing that except for the importance of oil, the issues there were only obscure foreign policy issues. But the horror and pain of the killings that recalled the historic attacks at Pearl Harbor and Normandy brought the Middle East home to America.

One thing became clear after the September 11 attacks: No consensus exists about a definition of terrorism. Some argue that the definition is merely a matter of perspective. If one condemns a cause, then those who support it are terrorists; on the other hand, if one supports a cause, then those who fight for it are heroes or freedom fighters. According to this view, those who hijacked planes and used them as weapons against American civilians are only terrorists if one rejects their cause. But most who examine the phenomenon of terrorism separate the causes supported by terrorists from the methods they use. If this approach is taken, then terrorism cannot be defined solely by reference to political perspective. By separating the cause itself from the means chosen to advance the cause, one allows for the classic question to be asked: Does the end justify the means? Does any cause, no matter how compelling, allow for the kind of killing that took place on September 11?

The U.S. Department of Defense defines terrorism as "the unlawful use or threat of violence against individuals or property to coerce or to intimidate governments or societies, often to achieve political, religious, or ideological objectives."[1] This definition is useful, but it doesn't help to distinguish freedom fighters from terrorists. All revolutionaries, for example, make use of "unlawful" violence, since their goal is to overturn the existing source of law. All revolutions involve violations of the law, but not all violations of the law—even those that involve violence—would normally be identified as acts of terrorism. If the Department of Defense definition were to be accepted, then American patriots during the Revolutionary War would have to be called terrorists.

One possible way to examine the relationship between ends and means is to analyze the ways in which different groups pick their targets. Do freedom fighters and terrorists choose different kinds of targets? During World War II, there were several attempts by German officers to assassinate Hitler. Were these officers really terrorists? Most people would distinguish between an attack on a head of state who is responsible for policies considered to be offensive and an attack on a school child who is simply on his or her way home and happens by chance to be on a targeted bus. In the first case, the victim is seen (rightly or wrongly) as actually guilty of something. He or she is doing something specific that is found to be hateful by those who carry out the attack. In the second case, the school child is seen—even by the attackers—as innocent.

An alternative definition of terrorism emerges as these issues are considered, one which holds that the crucial distinction between freedom fighters and terrorists is in the choice of target. In other words, it is not sufficient to note that people have been killed or that people have been frightened. Both freedom fighters and terrorists take lives and cause fear. Terrorism cannot be identified by labeling it as "cowardly." Calling terrorists cowardly is convenient because cowardice is a despised quality, but some terrorists are quite brave, especially if they give their lives for a cause in which they believe.

Freedom fighters attack those they identify as enemies; terrorists attack the innocent in order to pursue broad goals they find important. The victims are really incidental to the process. In a sense, the victims are necessary to advertise the chosen cause, but there is no particular reason that one person should die any more than another. If this distinction stands up to scrutiny, then a better definition of terrorism would be the killing of the innocent to make a political statement.

If we apply this tentative definition to recent political events, it seems clear that not all attacks on the United States that have been labeled as terrorist acts really qualify as such. For example, when the *U.S.S. Cole* was attacked in October, 2000, as it was refueling in a Yemen port, 17 American servicemen were killed and 39 were wounded. The United States called this an act of terrorism, and yet it was an attack on our military by people who wanted to eliminate the American military presence in the region. The attack was a sneak attack, but American revolutionaries did not always play fair when they sought to kill British soldiers during the Revolutionary War. Freedom fighters sometimes engage in sneak attacks. Those who attacked the American ship saw the American military (rightly or wrongly) as the enemy.

In the bombing of the Murrah Federal Building in Oklahoma City in April of 1995, 168 people were killed and 600 were wounded. Although those who were responsible had some general complaints against the U.S. government, there was no direct connection between their complaints and their target. Some of the people at the Federal Building were federal employees, but some were not. Surely the children at the building's day care center were not guilty of any crimes that made them legitimate targets for death. The choice of victims was incidental. In the case of the September 11 attacks, it does not seem to have been important to the terrorists who was on the hijacked planes or who was in the buildings that were attacked. The important thing was to carry out the attacks and to cause sufficient loss of life to make a political statement.

It is important to stress that the political statement being made may not be clear to the general public, especially if the terrorist group responsible for the attack does not claim responsibility. In the last few years, this has happened with increasing frequency. One of the reasons is that modern law-enforcement agencies have developed sophisticated methods for tracking down terrorists. Terrorist groups might pay too heavy a price for taking credit for an attack. No one claimed responsibility for the September 11 attacks; even so, the American government identified a group as responsible and waged what was essentially a war to punish those responsible and to render their organization useless. Self-interest might demand that terrorist groups not take credit for their actions. Also, sometimes it is more ominous to leave responsibility vague; a political point can be made even if responsibility is never taken for an attack. Finally, some groups are content if a small circle of like-minded people know who carried out an attack. This has been called "rage terrorism," which is violence provoked by a general sense of anger against a threatening world.

Any attempt to define terrorism must confront the question: When did terrorism begin? Is it simply a modern phenomenon, or is there a long tradition that informs and inspires contemporary terrorists? Throughout history, people have often turned to violence to achieve their goals. In ancient times, tyrannicide was an accepted if controversial doctrine that justified the murder of those in power who were seen as a threat to justice. The murder of Julius Caesar was carried out by respectable citizens who believed that they had an obligation to end his life to protect Rome. They did not see themselves as criminals, but as honorable men, as Shakespeare's Antony would later call them.

When does tyrannicide end and terrorism begin? A group known as the Assassins emerged in the eleventh century in Iran; they advanced the art of murder to a new level and are often seen as the first terrorists. After the Prophet Muhammad died, an argument within the Islamic community developed over who should succeed him. Many were unhappy with the choice of Abu Bakr as caliph (or deputy) and believed that Ali, the cousin and son-in-law of Muhammad should have been chosen. This group became known as the party of Ali, or the Shi'a. The Shi'a turned to the religious authority of the imam, or rightful head of Islam, as a kind of competitor to the Caliphs. A break within the Shi'a faction took place following the death of the sixth imam after Ali; most of the Shi'a recognized Musa al-Kazim as the seventh imam. This line of imams continued until the twelfth disappeared in 873. According to the tradition, the twelfth imam is the Hidden Imam, who will return someday as the savior (or Mahdi) to bring justice to the world. Twelver Shi'ism is the official religion of Iran today.

A minority of Shi'a believed that Musa's older brother Isma'il should have been chosen as the imam. The group called the Assassins developed from this particular sect of the Shi'a party of Islam known as the Ismailis. They fought to promote their version of Shi'a Islam, and they were attacked and in their eyes persecuted for their quest. They murdered their victims by a knife, which became the weapon of choice for the Assassins. They identified their targets as enemies of the religion, and those who took the lives of enemies were praised for their devotion to the cause. The crucial fact to remember about the Assassins is that they chose specific victims who were responsible for attacks on their group. They focused their attention on two main groups: princes and other political leaders who supported the rival Sunni group; and religious leaders who had spoken out against them in public. The Ismaili attacks were directed against specific people considered to be dangerous to their religious group.[2] This is important. An ordinary Sunni had nothing to fear from the Assassins. The terror they inspired was focused only on those who attempted to suppress. They did not attempt to foster generalized or indiscriminate terror. Were the Assassins terrorists? Some would say they were, and reasonable arguments can be advanced to support this view. But the care with which they chose their targets suggests that the political murders they carried out were not acts of terrorism. In fact, it is difficult to identify systematic killing of the innocent for political purposes until the modern age. When did people begin to see life as so dispensable? Is there something characteristic of modernity that inspires a new approach to killing? These are questions for which there are no easy answers.

There seem to be three main categories of contemporary terrorism that can be described without denying the possibility that other categories might be recognized. Since the phenomenon of terrorism is complex, any attempt to develop categories for the purposes of study is in some sense artificial. It imposes order and clarity on a subject that in many ways defies order and clarity, but these three categories can serve as an introduction to the topic.

RELIGIOUSLY MOTIVATED TERRORISM

This category of terrorism is characterized by a group's identification of its actions with religious doctrine. The group itself could be quite wrong in its interpretation of religion. One of the problems in identifying terrorist groups as religiously motivated is that religion can be misrepresented or used quite cynically by groups to recruit or motivate rank and file members. The problem with the term "Muslim Fundamentalist" has already been discussed. It suggests that Islam, properly or strictly interpreted, leads to terrorism. This is very misleading. Osama bin Laden claims that his group represents Islam, and yet Islamic representatives from around the world condemned the September 11 attacks on the United States. Does HAMAS really represent Islam? Clearly, many in the organization believe that it does, yet HAMAS has claimed responsibility for some acts of violence that have targeted innocent civilians and nothing in Islam allows for the intentional killing of the innocent. In a sense, the term "Religiously Motivated Terrorism" is misleading. Religion plays a role in these terrorist groups, but the version of religion active in these cases may, in fact, be driven by nonreligious or antireligious motives.

Many terrorist groups use the cover of religion to pursue their political goals. This chapter will focus on Al-Qaida and HAMAS, two of the most important terrorist organizations active at this time. Al-Qaida is the group thought to be responsible for the September 11, 2001, attacks on the United States, and HAMAS is the group currently challenging Yassir Arafat's Palestinian Authority in the West Bank and Gaza.

Al-Qaida

Al-Qaida means "The Base," and was conducting its operations from Afghanistan, where it was sheltered by the Taliban government until the United States began its military strikes as part of its War on Terrorism. The organization grew out of the 1979 Afghan war against the Soviet Union, and many of its members are veterans of that war. One of the great ironies of recent history is that Saudi Arabia and the United States both financed and armed Afghan rebel groups at that time, unwittingly providing a foundation for what was later to become Al-Qaida. The organization was founded in 1988 by Osama bin Laden, originally from Saudi Arabia. Bin Laden is himself wealthy, with estimated assets of over $300 million. His organization is well funded by businesses he owns, many of which are based in the Sudan. These businesses include construction and trucking companies and a variety of investment schemes. In addition, Al-Qaida is suspected of being behind a very successful drug trade. The United Nations has accused the organization of selling highly addictive liquid heroin in the West. Using sophisticated technology it can easily afford, Al-Qaida coordinates activities in approximately 55 nations. Al-Qaida is known to try to produce chemical weapons and to obtain nuclear weapons.

Its main goals are to strengthen Islam as it understands it by supporting the destruction of what it considers to be heretical Islamic states and to destroy the United States, which it sees as the leading exporter of moral corruption and political oppression in the world. A simple division of the world into good and bad lies behind Al-Qaida's activities. The world seems to be divided into believers and heretics. The heretics include Muslim states such as Saudi Arabia, which bin Laden believes has betrayed the religion, and the United States, which is guilty of threatening the holy sites in Mecca and Medina. Bin Laden sees Israel as an American surrogate and is therefore identified as one of his targets. In his "Declaration of War against the Americans Occupying the Land of the Two Holy Places," he says that "the latest and the greatest of [the] aggressions, incurred by the Muslims since the death of the Prophet . . . is the occupation of the land of the two Holy Places . . . by the armies of the American Crusaders and their allies."

It is important to understand that bin Laden's concerns are not related primarily to specific policy stands of countries like Saudi Arabia and the United States. These countries are, at their core, fundamentally corrupt (from his perspective), which is why he does not seek to improve them through accepted, peaceful means. In 1998, bin Laden formed an umbrella organization for terrorist groups called The Islamic World Front for the Struggle against the Jews and the Crusaders, which included representation from al-Gama's al-Islamiyya and al-Jihad.[3] It is important to note the reference to Western powers as crusaders; clearly a sense of history informs Al-Qaida. The wrongs suffered by Muslims during the Crusades still weigh heavily on the group's consciousness. It was unfortunate that

President Bush began his campaign against international terrorism by calling it a Crusade; this, in a sense, supported bin Laden's interpretation of world events. President Bush soon dropped the term once he understood how it was understood. For many in the West, the term has become a general one associated with any significant effort, but for many in the Middle East, the Crusades continue to be a living event. This is one more way in which problems are layered in the region, making the pursuit of peace more difficult.

Al-Qaida's vision is extreme and excludes the possibility of compromise, which is one of the things that makes the organization so dangerous. A senior fellow at the Center for Strategic and International Studies in Washington, D.C., explains that "They believe that their violence is divinely justified, and that great goals require dramatic means, and the dramatic means is mass bloodshed."[4] Among the many acts of terrorism attributed to Al-Qaida before the dramatic attacks on New York and Washington, D.C., on September 11, 2001, are the 1993 bombing of the World Trade Center, which killed six and wounded 1,000, and the attacks on the U.S. embassies in Kenya and Tanzania in 1998, which resulted in the deaths of 224, with 5,000 wounded. A Sudanese group that killed 58 tourists in Egypt in 1997 was probably working with bin Laden. The organization is also thought to be behind the attacks on the U.S. base in Dhahran, Saudi Arabia, in 1996, where 19 soldiers were killed and 372 wounded, and on the *USS Cole* in 2000, where 17 were killed and 39 wounded. These attacks do not necessarily qualify as acts of terrorism, as has already been discussed. Bin Laden has chosen both civilian and military targets over the years; the suggestion of this chapter is that attacks on military targets—as terrible and as unfair as they might be—can be condemned in many ways, but these attacks are not examples of terrorism.

The attack on the World Trade Center on September 11, 2001, defines Al-Qaida as one of the most ruthless and dangerous terrorist organizations in the world. Almost 3,000 were killed that day, when four planes full of innocent people were hijacked and used as weapons. In New York, 343 firefighters and 23 police officers who were attempting to help the victims were among those killed. One business in the World Trade Center lost 700 employees, leaving over 50 pregnant widows. Even countries critical of the United States condemned the attacks on civilians as brutal acts of terrorism.

HAMAS

HAMAS means zeal, and it is an acronym for the Islamic Resistance Movement. It grew out of the Muslim Brotherhood, which is one of the most powerful and well-established Islamic political organizations in the Middle East. Sheikh Ahmad Yassin, who had been a leader in the Muslim Brotherhood, was instrumental in founding HAMAS in 1980 and has been its leader since. One of the things that distinguishes HAMAS from Al-Qaida is that a significant amount of its work is social in nature. It supervises a number of charity organizations in Gaza and the West Bank, and is responsible for employing thousands of Palestinians in work that is in no way related to terrorism. This has enhanced the reputation of HAMAS among Palestinians and helped it to challenge the Palestinian Authority. Some scholars have gone as far as to deny that HAMAS is a terrorist organization, suggesting that it is "essentially a social movement" which has "directed its energies and resources primarily toward providing services to the community, especially responding to its immediate hardships and concerns."[5] One of the largest of the charity organizations operated by HAMAS is the Islamic Society, which supports Palestinian orphans, provides funding for Palestinian kindergartens, and sends subsidies to indigent families. A second is the Holy Land Foundation, a Texas-based organization that provided food handouts to the poor until its assets were frozen by President Bush in December of 2001 because he believed that charity funds were being funneled to terrorist activities. Many Palestinians say that HAMAS does more for the average Palestinian than Arafat and the Palestinian Authority. When Arafat closes down HAMAS offices in order to show that he is fighting terrorism, many Palestinians think that he is collaborating with the Israelis.

HAMAS also has a military section called The Palestinian Holy Fighters, and this group has been responsible for some of the most shocking terrorist attacks in the Middle East. In 1994, it used a car bomb to attack a bus in Afula, Israel. Eight people were killed, including a 13-year old, a 17-year old, and two teachers. Fifty-one others were also injured in the attack. In 1996, a suicide bomber blew up a bus in Jerusalem, killing 26 and injuring 80 others. In three separate attacks on marketplaces in 1997, 34 were killed and 529 were injured. A dramatic set of coordinated attacks in early December of 2001 left 26 dead and hundreds wounded in Israel. The victims were young people in a shopping and entertainment area and people riding on a bus, and one of the bombs was timed to kill rescue workers on their way to treat the victims. HAMAS has also attacked people on the street and in restaurants by firing on them from moving vehicles. It is clear from the character of these attacks that they qualify as acts of terrorism under the definition offered in this chapter. HAMAS did not kill these people because they were guilty of anything. The dramatic killings were designed to draw attention to the cause HAMAS supported.

The goals of HAMAS are stated openly in its Covenant, published in 1988. According to the document, the organization is a blend of religion and politics: "The Islamic Resistance Movement draws its guidelines from Islam." Its ultimately political goal is to destroy all of Israel and to replace it with what HAMAS would consider to be a legitimate Islamic state. "The Islamic Resistance Movement is a distinct Palestinian movement which . . . strives to raise the banner of Allah over every inch of Palestine." HAMAS therefore differs from the old PLO and the newer Palestinian Authority, which claim to be interested in making peace with Israel and establishing a secular state on only part of what used to be known as Palestine.

There is a curious undercurrent to the Covenant, which contributes to its ominous tone. Jews rather than Israelis are often identified as the enemy. "Our struggle against the Jews is extremely wide-ranging and grave, so much so that it will need all the loyal efforts we can wield." The Covenant is also informed by rather unusual conspiracy theories that draw on themes that have defined as traditional antisemitism. According to the document, Jews are a wealthy elite that have used their money to ruin the world. "This wealth allowed them to take over control of the world media such as news agencies, the press, publication houses, broadcasting and the like." The Jews, according to the Covenant, have used their wealth "to take over control of the Imperialist states and [make] them colonize many countries in order to exploit the wealth of these countries and spread their corruption therein." Most amazingly, Jews are seen as the secret, dangerous force behind what are identified as "destructive spying organizations," such as Rotary Clubs, Lions Clubs, Free Masons, and B'nai B'rith.

HAMAS makes it clear in the Covenant that violence is essential to its program. It explicitly rejects "peace initiatives, the so-called peaceful solutions, and international conferences." The reason for this is that unbelievers cannot be trusted: "Since when did the Unbelievers do justice to the Believers"? HAMAS identifies violence against unbelievers as a religious duty for all Muslims, until such time as Islam rules everywhere. In other words, it is part of the HAMAS world vision to shun peace, and that world vision is defined by a particular interpretation of religion.

POLITICALLY MOTIVATED TERRORISM

This type of terrorism is inspired by secular, political goals. The group in question kills innocent people in order to win freedom from a ruling group. It hopes that its activities will call attention to the plight of the oppressed, as it understands oppression. One group often identified as a terrorist group was the Jewish group, the Irgun (National Military Organization), which fought both Arabs and the British in order to promote an independent Israel, but which had no religious goals whatsoever. What was known as the PLO (Palestine Liberation Organization) sought to develop an independent state on land controlled by Israel. Terrorism committed by the PLO (before Yassir Arafat renounced violence and formed the Palestinian Authority) was not designed to advance Islam in any way, and the PLO did not have as one of its goals the creation of a state ruled by Islamic law. In fact, this was one of the sources of tension between HAMAS and the PLO. Arafat has never pursued the goal of an Islamic state. The goals or ends for politically motivated terrorists are freedom and territory. The means they employ are what identify them as terrorists.

The PLO was important to the historical development of the Palestinian people and is emphasized here because of the important role that it has played in recent history, but the Jewish group known as the Irgun (like the PLO, but no longer in existence) was also important in the creation of the state of Israel and is considered by many to be a terrorist group. During the final years of the British occupation of Palestine, the Irgun carried out a number of violent activities, including the bombing of the King David Hotel in July of 1946, which held the headquarters of the British occupation force. Ninety-one people were killed in the explosion. Most importantly, the Irgun was responsible for a bloody attack on the community of Deir Yassin in April of 1948 that claimed the lives of over 200 Arab men, women, and children. Many scholars have argued that the Irgun carried out the attack to frighten the Arab population in the area to flee. The leader of the Irgun, Menachem Begin, has always denied that the attacks were terrorist attacks or that the Irgun targeted innocent people, but the incident has become legendary and is often cited as an act of Jewish terrorism. The fact that

Begin was later elected as prime minister has always been resented by Palestinians, who see this as a confirmation of Israeli endorsement of terror as a weapon.

The PLO was one of a number of radical groups founded in the Middle East during the 1960s. Ahmad al-Shuqairi, the former representative of Saudi Arabia to the United Nations, was its first leader. Yassir Arafat took over leadership of the PLO in 1969, with his Fatah organization taking a leading role in its activities. Arafat was in control of the PLO through the creation of the PA (Palestinian Authority), but the PLO always included competing groups and rival leaders interested in promoting themselves. Because a number of different factions always existed within the PLO, some ambiguity has always existed about terrorist actions ascribed to it. In some cases it seems reasonable to admit that terrorist actions were carried out without the authorization of its leadership. The existence of these factions also allowed the PLO to deny responsibility for some actions that were authorized.

The PLO Charter announced what the goals of the organization were: "Palestine is the homeland of the Arab Palestinian people; it is an indivisible part of the Arab homeland." This is an important but potentially confusing statement, because the term "Palestine" is ambiguous, as was discussed in the Introduction. In the Second Article of the Charter, Palestine is defined by "the boundaries it had during the British Mandate." The PLO's conception of Palestine includes all of Israel and Jordan. This would mean that the goals of the PLO included the destruction of all of Israel and Jordan. It is important to recognize that while many connected to the PLO were believing Muslims, the goals of the PLO were completely secular. The PLO existed to work for the establishment of a Palestinian state that was never defined in religious terms.

Like HAMAS, the PLO openly stated that "armed struggle is the only way to liberate Palestine." Peace agreements can only be used as tactical moves to gain immediate benefits. The PLO sometimes acted alone in carrying out its terrorist activities, but it also recruited people from outside the organization to carry out violent attacks that were consistent with its goals. Attacks on airlines became popular because they were relatively vulnerable and because the attacks received so much media attention. The PLO sponsored the hijacking of planes and the machine-gun killings of passengers and crew members on planes to and from the Middle East in the late 1960s and 1970s. The most dramatic example of this was in September of 1970, when four planes (Swissair, PanAM, TWA, and BOAC) carrying 310 civilian passengers were hijacked and flown to a desert landing site in Jordan. The passengers were later released, partly because of concessions from various governments, and partly because King Hussein of Jordan launched a major attack on PLO strongholds on the West Bank that same month.[6] In 1972, a group with ties to the PLO sent operatives to the Munich Olympics and murdered 11 Israeli athletes. Some of the terrorists were killed in a battle with the police, but those who survived were later released by the German government, apparently to secure the release of other German hostages. These activities fall within the definition of terrorism offered in this chapter. The athletes were not political or military figures, and the Olympics is a nonpolitical event designed to bring together people from different parts of the world to meet in friendly athletic competition. The athletes were targets because their deaths would advertise the plight of the Palestinians, not because the victims themselves were seen as guilty of anything.

There have been two major military assaults on the PLO. As has already been mentioned, the King of Jordan attacked PLO camps in September of 1970, killing thousands in an event now known as Black September. Hussein was responding to what he believed was a threat to his country. The PLO had established what was essentially its own substate, collecting their own taxes, printing their own license plates for cars, and recruiting young men to join their forces. In 1982, the Israelis attacked the PLO's new home in Beirut, Lebanon, in a move that resulted in international condemnation of Israel. The military action by the Israelis broke the military strength of the PLO, but it also created a new level of sympathy for the Palestinian cause.

Over the years, the PLO developed an official status as the representative of the Palestinian people, and it took on more legitimate responsibilities. By the 1980s, the PLO employed over 8,000 in jobs not related to terrorism, making it an important social as well as political force. It supported a number of hospitals and clinics, job training centers, and educational programs. After the Oslo Peace Agreement was signed in 1993, the PLO formally renounced terrorism and made a commitment to remove the sections of its Charter that called for the destruction of Israel. This paved the way for the transition to the Palestinian Authority, which has taken the place of the old terrorist organization.

STATE-SPONSORED TERRORISM

This form of terrorism is characterized by attacks by a government on its own citizens or on international targets that are sponsored in one way or another by a government. One could argue that Hitler's attack on the Jews was a form of state terrorism. Hitler did not seek to find Jews who were guilty of crimes against the state. The mere fact that they were alive made them targets of state action. The Serb attacks on Muslims in Bosnia in the 1990s could also be cited as examples of state terrorism. The Muslims who were targeted were not charged with crimes or identified as enemies; they were killed only because of their religious identity. State terrorism often has secular goals, even when its acts of terrorism are directed against religious groups. Hitler, for example, was not promoting Christianity when he set the Final Solution into motion, even though he drew on religious prejudice against Jews to gain support for his programs. Some countries such as Syria have provided funding for and shelter to a variety of terrorist groups, in the hope that these groups will advance the goals of the state, which may be quite different from the goals of the groups they sponsor.

Seven countries are currently on the State Department's list of state sponsors of terrorism: Iran, Iraq, Syria, Libya, Cuba, North Korea, and the Sudan. It is interesting to note that Afghanistan did not make it onto this list, yet it is the country that sheltered and supported Al-Qaida. As an example, this section will focus on the example of Syria, which has a long tradition of sponsoring terrorist organizations.

The Syrians have provided support to approximately 30 percent of the groups on the State Department's list of state-sponsored terrorist organizations. These groups include Hizbollah, HAMAS, the Popular Front for the Liberation of Palestine, and the Kurdistan Workers' Party. A number of the leaders of these organizations live in Syria and have their training bases, political bases, and propaganda offices in Damascus. For example, HAMAS and Islamic Jihad have been operating openly in Syria and have their offices in Damascus. Much of the leadership of HAMAS and Islamic Jihad responsible for planning terrorist activities carries out its activities in Syria. In addition, the military and political infrastructure of a number of terrorist organizations is set up in areas of Lebanon controlled by Syria. In other words, Syria offers its support to groups that need assistance but does not officially control the organizations. Syria hopes that its assistance will be rewarded by cooperation with the terrorist groups it sponsors and that it can encourage operations against Israel, provide a counterpoint to Arafat's leadership of the Palestinians, and maintain control of important sections of Lebanon. Many terrorist attacks in the Middle East against Western targets in the 1980s and 1990s were made possible by Syrian support, including the killing of 241 American troops in 1983 at the Marine base in Beirut, designed to force the Americans to leave Lebanon. Syria's approach has been to cooperate with Iran to allow for funding and support of groups such as Hizbollah through Syria; in this way, Syria maintains some ability to deny involvement in terrorist activities. Syria allows groups like Hizbollah to operate in areas of Lebanon under its control and makes it possible for weapons and ammunition to be sent from Iran to terrorist groups through the Damascus International Airport, where Iranian shipments do not face any form of inspection. In other words, Syria could easily cut of what one scholar has called Hizbollah's "life line."[7]

State-sponsored terrorism is significant because many terrorist groups do not have the resources to remain active on their own. Recent events have shown that groups such as Al-Qaida depend on the shelter provided by states and are significantly impaired when that shelter is removed. State-sponsored terrorism is an important resource for countries such as Syria, as Bruce Hoffman has explained:

> For all seven of the countries identified by the State Department, then, terrorism remains a useful and integral tool of their respective foreign policies: a clandestine weapon to be wielded whenever the situation is appropriate and the benefits palpable, but remaining sheathed when the risks of using it appear to outweigh the potential gains and the possible repercussions are likely to prove counterproductive. . . .[8]

Hoffman points out that states sponsor terror in order to secure what he calls 'surrogate warriors,' and that one lesson of the Gulf War may be that overt action by states is more dangerous than sponsoring terrorists. It remains to be seen if U.S. military action against the Taliban regime in Afghanistan in 2001 and 2002 will alter this equation and encourage states to distance themselves from terrorist groups that have been helpful to them in the past.

Selected Bibliography

Esposito, John, *The Islamic Threat: Myth or Reality* (New York: Oxford University Press, 1992).

Hoffman, Bruce, *Inside Terrorism* (New York: Columbia University Press, 1998).

Mishal, Ahaul, and Sela, Avraham, *The Palestinian HAMAS: Vision, Violence, and Coexistence* (New York: Columbia University Press, 2000).

Endnotes

1. Bruce Hoffman, *Inside Terrorism* (New York: Columbia University Press, 1998), 38.

2. See Bernard Lewis, *The Assassins* (New York: Oxford University Press, 1967), 125. My discussion of the assassins draws heavily on this respected historical analysis.

3. See the International Policy Institute for Counter-Terrorism at www.ict.org.il.

4. Karen DeYoung and Michael Dobbs, "The Architect of a New Global Terrorism," *Washington Post National Weekly Edition,* vol. 18, no. 48, 20.

5. Shaul Mishal and Avraham Sela, *The Palestinian HAMAS: Vision, Violence, and Coexistence* (New York: Columbia University Press, 2000), vii.

6. Howard Sachar, *A History of Israel* (New York: Alfred Knopf, 1979), 633, 686, 699.

7. Dr. Reuven Ehrlich, ICT Research Fellow, www.ict.org.il.

8. Hoffman, 195.

Chapter 10

The Peace Process and the Future

In the final days of his term of office, President Clinton made one last attempt to use American influence to conclude an agreement between Israelis and Palestinians on the issues that had produced so much conflict for so many years. But the series of negotiations that had produced a tentative framework for discussions back in 1993 seemed to be in real trouble. What had become known as the Peace Process appeared to be unraveling.

Fighting in the streets in the West Bank and Gaza had been severe and by January of 2001 over 300 people had been killed; the level of anger among Israelis and Palestinians was rising quickly. Palestinians were proclaiming a new *intifada*, HAMAS was calling for "days of rage" against the Israelis every Friday, and Israel's Prime Minister Barak had to resign and call for new elections amidst a flurry of accusations from conservatives in the government that his concessions to Palestinian demands had in some way encouraged the violence. Every day people were dying in confrontations between rock-throwing Palestinians and Israeli soldiers, in violent gun battles between newly armed Palestinians (including Palestinian police who joined in the street fighting) and Israelis, and in terrorist attacks against civilians on buses and in city markets. What had happened to the Peace Process?

Some argued that promising peace initiatives had been derailed by extremists on both sides. Others suggested that while the Israelis and Palestinians wanted peace, American efforts to produce an agreement put unacceptable pressure on the process and led to increased tensions. An increasing number of voices began to articulate a disturbing theory, that the Peace Process was always a fraud and that its collapse was inevitable. This chapter will discuss the major events in the Peace Process and analyze the challenges to peace in the future.

THE OSLO ACCORDS OF 1993

No major progress had been made toward peace in the Middle East since the Camp David Accords of 1978 and the treaty between Israel and Egypt in 1979, but in 1991, negotiations seemed to head in a promising direction when Israeli and Palestinian (but not formally PLO) teams agreed to meet directly to discuss peace at a conference in Madrid. The international climate was an important contributing factor to the new willingness to negotiate.[1] The Soviet Union was in the process of disintegrating, which meant that the Cold War was over and those rejecting peace in the Middle East could not fall back on Soviet support. The United States, on the other hand, had just led a powerful coalition (including a number of Arab states) against Saddam Hussein in the Gulf War. It was the one remaining superpower and President Bush believed that a "New World Order" was emerging that was ripe with possibilities for peace.

There were, however, many obstacles remaining. The Israeli government defied the United States by continuing to establish new Jewish settlements in the West Bank, and the PLO defied the United States by publicly supporting Saddam Hussein during the Gulf War. President Bush attempted to use the new strength and prestige of the United States to put pressure on both sides. In 1992, Bush refused to give American support to loan guarantees that Israel was seeking to address financial problems that were arising as a result of a new wave of immigration from the former Soviet Union. Bush linked support for the $10 billion in loan guarantees to a promise from the Israeli government to cease all settlements on the West Bank. Bush also took a hard line with the PLO, demanding that they renounce violence and agree to settle differences with Israel through negotiation. He also encouraged Arab governments to reconsider their support of the PLO because of the PLO's support of Iraq in the Gulf War. By 1992, the PLO felt increasingly isolated and was having serious financial problems.

The new aggressiveness of the United States may have given encouragement to the Labor Party in Israel, which took over the government of Israel in 1992. New Prime Minister Yitzhak Rabin was more willing to consider the American perspective than his conservative predecessor, Yitzhak Shamir. Rabin agreed to stop all plans for new settlements, and he expressed a willingness to meet directly with representatives of the PLO, a group that had not formally renounced terrorism and that still called for the destruction of Israel in its Charter. President Bush finally agreed to support the loan guarantees, much to the disappointment of Palestinians, who believed that too few concessions had been extracted from the Israelis.

In spite of American aggressiveness in pursuit of its particular vision of peace in the Middle East, or perhaps partly because of it, the first real breakthrough came from a surprising direction. A representative from a Norwegian peace institute, Foreign Minister Johan Jorgen Holst, established contacts with Israeli government officials and members of the PLO and became convinced that enough common ground existed to make meaningful negotiations possible. Secret talks were held in Norway, and in 1993, a dramatic agreement was reached. Israel agreed to recognize the PLO as the legitimate representative of the Palestinian people, and the PLO agreed to recognize Israel's right to exist. A Declaration of Principles was also produced, which established a framework for further negotiations. Israel agreed to support increasing Palestinian autonomy in the West Bank and Gaza, as long as the PLO continued to support peace and Israel's security was not threatened. A five-year period was set for this process of incremental withdrawal of Israeli troops from the areas of Palestinian autonomy. At the end of this five-year period, a final agreement would be signed in accordance with U.N. Resolutions 242 and 338. At this time, the Accords envisioned a new, elected Palestinian Council with the power of taxation that would take on responsibility for a number of domestic tasks, including education and social welfare. The Olso Accords held out the promise of a lasting peace, stating:

> The Government of the State of Israel and the Palestinian team . . . representing the Palestinian people, agree that it is time to put an end to decades of confrontation and conflict, recognize their mutual legitimate and political rights, and strive to live in peaceful coexistence and mutual dignity and security and achieve a just, lasting and comprehensive peace settlement and historic reconciliation through the agreed political process.[2]

The Oslo Accords were dramatic but tentative. Each side believed that its compliance with the agreement was linked to the commitment of the other side to fulfill its part of the bargain. Israel did not believe that it was obligated to continue withdrawal from the West Bank and Gaza if the PLO returned to violence, and the PLO did not believe that its renunciation of violence was binding if Israel refused to continue its withdrawal.

Seeds were sown for future conflict by the fact that three of the most contentious issues were simply postponed for later discussion. First of all, the status of Jerusalem was not addressed. Most Palestinians wanted part of Jerusalem as the capital of the emerging Palestinian state, but Israel considered Jerusalem to be its capital. This issue was political and religious, since a number of sites holy to both Muslims and Jews are in Jerusalem. Second, the issue of refugees was postponed. Palestinians claimed a right of return for those they claimed had been driven from their land in 1948 (and for their decedents, now numbering in the millions). Israel believed it would face possible disintegration if a hostile population of that size were to be introduced to the country. Finally, Israel had only endorsed limited autonomy in Oslo, but it was clear that the Palestinians saw the Accords as a transitional step to complete sovereignty and a new Palestinian state.

In spite of its limitations, many saw the Oslo Accords (now known as Olso I) as a dramatic step toward peace. The United States was caught completely off guard by news of the agreement, but President Clinton recovered quickly and arranged to have the official signing on the White House lawn, where dramatic photographs were taken of the Prime Minister of Israel, Itzhak Rabin, shaking hands with Yassir Arafat, the head of the PLO. The United States reclaimed its leadership role in the Peace Process by backing a plan for financial assistance to the Palestinians at two Donors Conferences, at which a total of $6 billion dollars in aid was promised by the international community and the World Bank.[3] Over the next two years, some progress was made toward peace, but new complications also emerged. In 1994, Israel and Jordan signed a formal peace treaty, and President Clinton visited Syria in an attempt to encourage Assad to begin serious negotiations with Israel. But in 1995, Prime Minister Rabin was assassinated by a Jewish radical who was opposed to the Peace Process. In 1995, the Israelis and the Palestinians signed an Interim Agreement (known as Oslo II) giving the details of Israeli military withdrawal and the development of the Palestinian authority. Tensions continued as each side accused the other of a multitude of violations. The Israelis began construction of settlements again, and Arafat refused to crack down on HAMAS and other groups that continued to engage in terrorist activities.

Ambivalence among Israelis about the peace process led to a change of government in Israel in 1996. The conservative Likud Party returned to power with Binyamin Netanyahu as Prime Minister. Netanyahu had been an active critic of the Oslo Accords, and many saw his election as a setback for peace. Netanyahu always claimed to want peace and never argued that the Oslo Accords should be abandoned; he simply said that since, in his opinion, the Palestinians were not conforming to the promises they had made at Oslo, it would be rash for the Israeli government to fulfill its obligations in a unilateral manner. He claimed that all he wanted from the Palestinians was "reciprocity."[4] From the perspective of the Palestinians, Netanyahu's election was a disaster because Netanyahu pushed for more settlements on the West Bank and Gaza, and because he refused to acknowledge that the Oslo Accords were a framework for the establishment of a new Palestinian state.

THE WYE MEMORANDUM OF 1998

President Clinton asked Netanyahu and Arafat to join him at the Wye Plantation in Maryland to address the serious problems that had been holding the peace process back. The negotiations yielded an affirmation of the basic principles of the Oslo Accords without producing any new initiatives. In the nine-page document, Israel renewed its pledge to withdraw from more territory, and the Palestinians promised to combat terror, collect illegal weapons, and amend the PLO Charter as it had promised to do in 1993 so that it no longer called for the destruction of Israel. Netanyahu agreed to a 13 percent withdrawal as long as 3 percent of the territory would remain a nature reserve (for security reasons). A time line was built into the Memorandum that provided for the responsibilities of both sides "to be carried out in a parallel phased approach."[5] In a rather odd move, the CIA was given the job of determining whether or not the two sides were complying with the agreement.

As Cleveland has observed, "what was lacking in the Wye Accords was the spirit of a partnership for peace that had characterized the atmosphere of Oslo I."[6] Both Netanyahu and Arafat were already condemning the agreement by the time they returned home. Both were being subjected to increasing criticism from their political opponents. Netanyahu was condemned by conservatives who believed that he had conceded too much without demanding any real concessions from the Palestinians, and Arafat was condemned for allowing Israel to move too slowly on compliance with the Oslo Accords. Arafat had been promising the Palestinians that the peace process would yield autonomy first and then independence, but the five years envisioned by Oslo I had come and gone, and the Palestinians had neither autonomy nor independence.

The skeptical Netanyahu was replaced as Prime Minister by Ehud Barak of the Labor Party in 1999, and Barak took immediate steps to implement peace agreements already signed. In fact, he went further than was required and began an early withdrawal of troops from the Israeli security sector in southern Lebanon as a sign of good faith. Barak made it clear that he was just as concerned about security as Netanyahu, but he was an enthusiastic advocate of the Oslo Peace Process. He announced publicly that he favored a Palestinian state and that he was willing to discuss approaches to honoring the Palestinian request for the return of refugees. The stage was set for the next important summit to complete the Peace Process and begin the new century with a transformed Middle East.

THE FAILED CAMP DAVID SUMMIT OF 2000

President Clinton had high hopes when he invited Barak and Arafat to Camp David in July of 2000. From the perspective of the United States, the new prime minister of Israel was more flexible than any previous Israeli leader had ever been. He seemed open to all the traditional concerns of the Palestinian people, although it was clear that some flexibility was needed on both sides if a final agreement was to be reached. At the meeting, Barak promised to turn over almost all the remaining land in the West Bank and Gaza to Palestinian control, with Israel keeping temporary control of a small, largely unpopulated area. To the surprise of everyone, Barak announced that he would consider a divided Jerusalem, with East Jerusalem serving as the capital of the new Palestinian state and the holy sites under international supervision. Barak hoped that a small part of the Temple Mount could hold a synagogue for Jewish prayer. No Israeli Prime Minister had ever taken such a bold step. Arafat turned down the Israeli offer, saying that the Temple Mount in East Jerusalem had to be completely under Palestinian control, and he left the meeting without making a counterproposal of any kind. President Clinton, who had been hoping to complete a Middle East peace treaty before he left office, was clearly disappointed with Arafat and expressed his frustration publicly.

Barak and Arafat met with increasing criticism from their own constituencies. Many Israelis were willing to accept the idea of a Palestinian state, but there was still strong opposition to a divided Jerusalem. When part of Jerusalem was under Jordanian control from 1948 to 1967, Jews were prohibited from praying at holy sites. What would happen if a Palestinian state controlled the Temple Mount, still thought of as the holiest site in Judaism? Arafat was being criticized by Palestinians who believed that he was too weak in negotiations, that he had been reduced to simply accepting any proposal made by an Israeli prime minister. The United States, from the perspective of the Palestinians, was not really neutral in these negotiations.[7]

The atmosphere was tense when the controversial Ariel Sharon (now back in politics after being censured for his role in the military action in Lebanon in 1982) visited the Temple Mount and proclaimed that Jews should always have the right to pray there. Violence broke out almost immediately as Palestinians who perceived this as a challenge to their claim to the Temple Mount went to the streets. A second *intifada* began, but this one was substantially more violent than the last, and hundreds of people were killed as the fighting continued for months. Even though more Palestinians had weapons now, and even though the

Palestinian police (now numbering approximately 40,000) were often involved in the fighting, the Israelis still had the upper hand in the conflict, and most of the casualties were Palestinian. Charges and countercharges were being made almost daily about who should accept responsibility for the violence. Was Ariel Sharon hoping to advance his political career by provoking the Palestinians to violence, or was Arafat encouraging his own people to engage in violent protest to take attention away from the failed Summit at Camp David?

THE AFTERMATH OF SEPTEMBER 11, 2001

The dynamics of the Peace Process changed dramatically after the September 11, 2001, terrorist attacks on the World Trade Center and the Pentagon. Americans felt more vulnerable than they had since *Sputnik* had first challenged the American feeling of invincibility in 1957. President George W. Bush identified terrorism as the primary threat to peace in the world, and he vowed to make the fight against terrorism the cornerstone of his administration. Then, as the United States was fighting against the Taliban regime of Afghanistan for harboring terrorism, terrorists struck in Israel in a dramatic attack on Passover that killed 29 and wounded 140 more. Ariel Sharon publicly compared Arafat to the Taliban, suggesting that Arafat was supporting groups like HAMAS and Islamic Jihad and announcing that Israel no longer considered Arafat to be a meaningful representative of the Palestinian people. Sharon called Arafat "irrelevant" and "the greatest obstacle to peace and security in the Middle East." Under the assumption that Arafat had the power to significantly reduce terrorism and was simply refusing to do so, the Israelis demanded that he arrest terrorists and shut down terrorist organizations. In order to emphasize their growing impatience, Sharon ordered the destruction of Arafat's helicopters and attacks on Palestinian police stations and Palestinian Authority headquarters. Because the dramatic attacks on Israel came shortly after the September 11 attacks on the United States, they were viewed differently in Washington. President Bush made it clear that he no longer accepted what he considered to be Arafat's excuses. The U.S. policy in the Middle East changed almost overnight. From an attempt to be honest brokers and work from a position of neutrality (perhaps never achieved) between the Israelis and the Palestinians, the United States made it clear that the future of the Peace Process depended entirely on Arafat's actions. Calls for Israeli restraint after terrorist attacks ended. Almost immediately, political leaders from around the world who had joined in condemning the September 11 attacks now criticized Arafat for not opposing terrorism with sufficient energy. Saudi Arabia, Jordan, Egypt, and Russia criticized Arafat as did Secretary General of the U.N. Kofi Annan.

As Arafat's position weakened, questions remained about whether he in fact had the power to crack down on terrorism. Was he harboring terrorism, or was his weak and sporadic opposition to it actually a reflection of his helplessness in the face of the growing popularity of HAMAS and Islamic Jihad? Some leaders, including Israeli Foreign Minister Shimon Peres, were concerned that removing Arafat from his leadership position would only result in the growing influence of radical elements. One problem is that the PA has no clear process for producing a successor to Arafat. A number of distinguished leaders have emerged in recent years, including Ahmed Qureia, the chief negotiator for the Oslo peace agreement, Mahmoud Abbas, the unofficial second-in-command of the PA, and Marwan Barghouti, the West Bank chief of Fatah. In the event that Arafat relinquished power or was driven from power, it is not clear who would take his place.

In an attempt to find new solutions to the tensions between the Israelis and the Palestinians, George W. Bush sent former U.S. Senator George Mitchell to represent the United States to a conference at Sharm el-Sheikh. The report, known as the Mitchell Report, was completed in April, 2001. It called for the government of Israel and the Palestinian Authority to act swiftly to end violence in order to set the stage for meaningful negotiations. Mitchell called for a cease-fire to establish what he called a meaningful "cooling off" period, a clear renunciation of violence, and an end to the construction of settlements in the West Bank and Gaza. The Mitchell Report was highly regarded at the time, and Secretary of State Colin Powell referred to it often in his public statements as the best hope for the future, but violence continued and negotiations seemed out of the question. In June, CIA Director George Tenet offered a plan to end the violence, a plan that was designed to provide a foundation for the goals set in the Mitchell Report. The plan called for a resumption of negotiations, but set as a precondition the successful completion of one week without attacks from the Palestinians or the Israelis. It called for the Palestinian Authority to take more aggressive action against the terrorist groups it claimed to condemn, and it required the Israelis to release all Palestinians arrested in the security sweeps it had conducted, provided that they were not accused of terrorist acts.

None of these efforts was successful. President Bush appeared before the United Nations to announce his support for a Palestinian state that would exist side-by-side with Israel, living peacefully with secure and recognized borders, and he continued to send representatives such as Colin Powell and Vice President Dick Cheney to the region. Early in 2002, Saudi Crown Prince Abdullah assumed a leadership role by proposing a new peace initiative. Following the outlines of an old 1949 proposal, he offered full recognition of Israel and normal relations for a return of all territory held since 1967 and full right of return for all Palestinians and their descendents who formerly lived in Israel. A fair amount of excitement was generated by the Saudi plan, and many hoped it would encourage a new beginning in the peace process. Israel did not respond positively; United Nations Resolution 242, which has been one of the foundational documents for negotiations, only states that Israel must return "territories" held since 1967. It does not require that "all" territories be returned. This small difference in wording might not seem significant at first, but from Israel's perspective, it removes all flexibility from a negotiated peace. Since there are now approximately 3 million refugees and descendents, it would be political suicide for Israel to allow them to return at this point. Some conservatives in the United States were skeptical about Saudi motives in promoting this plan, suggesting that the plan was an old one and clearly unworkable. Some conservative commentators even argued that the plan was designed to divert attention from the fact that almost all the terrorists who were implicated in the September 11 attacks on the United States were from Saudi Arabia. Indeed, as the plan was discussed, it was revealed that the government of

Saudi Arabia was currently sending money to support the families of suicide bombers. Saudi officials called this "humanitarian aid," but many were skeptical about the Saudi commitment to peace in light of this revelation.

Hopes for peace were frustrated again when the Israelis were accused by the Palestinians of slaughtering hundreds of innocent civilians in the refugee camp of Jenin in March, 2000. Palestinian sources claimed that over 500 people had been killed. The initial reports from the news media were sympathetic to this allegation, but investigations that followed confirmed that no massacre had taken place. Nonetheless, concern remained that Israeli forces had been responsible for an excessive number of civilian deaths. A United Nations report issued several months later stated that there was no massacre, but it criticized both the Palestinians and the Israelis for putting the lives of civilians at risk in the fighting that took place. The final figures on the number of dead are in dispute, but in August of 2002 the United Nations announced that there had been 52 Palestinians killed, along with the 23 Israeli soldiers who died in the fighting. Israeli officials claimed that Jenin was a center for terrorist activities and that the entire city was rigged with booby traps to protect terrorist centers. But the controversy over Jenin was not settled by the United Nations; many Palestinians still believe that a massacre took place and have taken up Jenin as a battle call for future action against the Israelis.

In the midst of so much violence, it is often difficult to sort out the facts and obtain a clear perspective. Many came to use the phrase "cycle of violence" to describe the situation. A terrorist attack by a Palestinian would presumably be designed to challenge what is seen as an oppressive Israeli occupation of the West Bank and Gaza; in other words, it is an act in response to Israeli action. After the terrorist attack (praised by some Palestinians and condemned by others), the Israelis engage in a limited military response, presumably to challenge the attacks on its own people. Often, a response to the response follows. But is this a "cycle of violence"? Is all violence equally likely to incite a response? Is all violence morally equal? These questions are difficult to answer in the middle of a conflict.

President Bush offered his first comprehensive statement on the Middle East in June of 2002. In a dramatic move that signaled his disillusionment with Arafat, Bush called on the Palestinian people to elect new leaders. After attempting to work with both the Israelis and the Palestinians without success since his election, Bush decided that Arafat was standing in the way of a true resolution of the conflict. Bush called for leaders "not compromised by terror," a clear allusion to Arafat. While it is true that Bush had been critical of the Israelis from time to time for reacting too quickly or too harshly to a specific incident, this speech condemned the Palestinian authorities for "encouraging, not opposing, terrorism." The speech also called for the Palestinians to create a functioning democracy based on tolerance and liberty. Once these things have taken place, Bush promised strong American support for a provisional Palestinian state that would achieve full sovereignty as part of a final peace settlement. One of the reasons for Bush's new tough stand on Arafat is that he has announced his plans to promote a "regime change" in Iraq. By the summer of 2002, his administration was looking at different options for toppling Saddam Hussein's government, believing it to be supporting terrorism and developing weapons of mass destruction. But the planned action against Iraq would be difficult if the Israelis and Palestinians were still in the middle of an intense conflict. Clearly, President Bush was interested in peace for its own sake, but the administration's need to focus on Iraq added urgency to Bush's Middle East initiatives.

While criticisms of the Peace Process grow after September 11, significant opposition to it among Israelis and Palestinians began shortly after Camp David. Perhaps there were fundamental assumptions inherent in the Oslo Accords that made genuine peace impossible. Even the term "Peace Process" was criticized; after all, it implied that the road to peace was fairly clear and that all that needed to be resolved were details. Although there are a multitude of perspectives on the Peace Process, there are two main criticisms that deserve special attention.

THE PALESTINIANS DO NOT WANT PEACE

This perspective is expressed most passionately by the conservative Jewish intellectual Norman Podhoretz, who is the editor-at-large of *Commentary* magazine. He argues that the second *intifada* is evidence of the fact that the Oslo Accords only promoted the illusion that peace was possible.

> The unbearable reality being evaded was that Israel's yearning for peace was shared neither by the Arab world in general nor by the Palestinians in particular—that their objection was not to anything Israel had done or failed to do, but to the very fact that it existed at all.[8]

Podhoretz criticizes Israeli leaders like Rabin and Peres (both of whom were awarded the Nobel Peace Prize along with Arafat) for failing to understand fundamental realities of the Middle East. The facts demonstrate that the Palestinians have never really renounced violence or terror, in spite of their promises at Oslo. Approximately twice as many Israelis were killed by suicide bombers in the three years after Oslo as were killed in the three years before. The 1996 violence that followed the opening of an archeological tunnel in Jerusalem is another example. Podhoretz says that the pattern is that the Palestinians will return to violence whenever it suits their purposes, and that they will use their children to create martyrs in order to influence world opinion.

According to this perspective, the Palestinians do not want their own country, they want to use the turmoil over their situation to wage an attack on Israel itself. As Podhoretz says, "they just want us out of the Middle East."[9] The fundamental truth obscured by infatuation with the Oslo Accords is that the "two-state" solution is nothing more than a temporary stage in what will become an all-out assault on Israel. Palestinians have a "strategy of stages" that will "more circuitously and cunningly head toward the same ultimate consummation in the destruction of the Jewish state." Podhoretz points to the fact that Palestinian textbooks for children contain maps on which Israel does not exist. Official Palestinian television (often not monitored by the American press or simply dismissed as full of harmless rhetoric) calls for *jihad* against the Jews, as does this excerpt of a sermon by Ahmad Abu Halabiya, former acting rector of the Islamic University in Gaza:

> Have no mercy on the Jews, no matter where they are, in any country. Fight them, wherever you are. Wherever you meet them, kill them. Wherever you are, kill those

Jews and those Americans who are like them and those who stand by them. They are all in one trench against the Arabs and the Muslims because they established Israel here, in the beating heart of the Arab world, in Palestine.[10]

There never has been a real Peace Process; the illusion has been kept alive by the naive hopes of those who sincerely wish for peace. Podhoretz argues that the creation of a Palestinian state in the West Bank and Gaza is only a stepping stone to further attacks on Israel. Arafat's unwillingness to combat terrorism is just another piece of evidence that he is not sincere about peace.

THE ISRAELIS DO NOT WANT PEACE

This perspective is presented by many, including the well-known advocate for a Palestinian state, Edward W. Said, a professor of English at Columbia University and the author of a number of books on Palestinian issues, including *The End of the Peace Process*. He says that the massive disparity in power between the Palestinians, on the one hand, and Israel linked with the United States on the other, means that a meaningful Palestinian state is virtually impossible. The purpose of the Peace Process is to contain and direct Palestinian aspirations and make them acceptable to Zionist and American imperial interests. He points out that it was actually Arafat's weakness as a political figure in 1992 that prompted Israelis to be interested in negotiating with him.[11] He says: "The disproportion in power between Israel and the Arabs is so great that there is no room for optimistic speculation of the kind that will suddenly make everyone happy."[12] There are, in his opinion, too many refugees still homeless, too many claims stemming from the expulsion from Israel in 1948, and too much of a commitment to discrimination against Palestinians to make the Oslo Accords anything more than a diversion. Said is even critical of Arafat for becoming a kind of stooge of the Israelis. "Arafat can be trusted to do the job of policing and demoralizing his people far better than the Israeli Civil Administration." While the Palestinians may have been hopeful in the early stages of the Peace Process, bitterness set in as real progress was not made. The only real outcome of the Peace Process is that the Israelis became more powerful; factional fighting broke out among the Palestinians that diverted attention for the struggle for freedom.[13]

The Israelis do not want real peace; they want to deny their past injustices and rush to a process of negotiations with the people most likely to conform to their interests. The goal of Oslo is to create the appearance of a movement toward Palestinian rights while allowing Israel to hold on to the real power and avoid admissions of guilt or real concessions. The Wye Memorandum is particularly repulsive, according to Said. From his perspective, Arafat gave away any hope of true Palestinian independence there. "Arafat and company have now completely delivered themselves to the combined Israeli and U.S. intelligence apparatus, thereby putting an end to anything even resembling a democratic and independent Palestinian national life."[14] The real winner at Wye was Israel, which promoted its security concerns without making a single, meaningful concession. The agreement succeeded only in continuing to "devalue and debase Palestinian life." In other words, the so-called Peace Process is supported by Israel and the United States because it suits their interests. The illusion of a Palestinian state may be created, but true peace is not possible or desirable under these conditions. The Israeli response to terrorism after September 11 is simply a tactic; Israel creates conditions that are intolerable for the Palestinians, which forces them to respond with force, and then the force they use is presented to the world as proof that they do not want peace.

The future of the Peace Process is in grave doubt. Will the fundamental disagreements that divide Israel and the Palestinians lead to another regional war, or will the outbursts of violence dissipate and will meaningful negotiations continue? Many still hope that the Peace Process can be brought "back on track," but as Podhoretz and Said have shown, some believe that the process itself is fundamentally corrupt. Does it mask a Palestinian desire to move beyond a demand for an independent state and head toward an attack on Israel? Or does it conceal an Israeli and American partnership to minimize the Palestinian people, to control their aspirations by manipulating an ineffective Palestinian leadership?

The problems facing the Peace Process are really a microcosm of the problems in the Middle East as a whole. Radically different perspectives on the basic historical facts and the broad political and religious principles of the people continue to make it difficult for true peace to emerge.

Selected Bibliography

Dajani, Souad, *Eyes Without Country* (Philadelphia: Temple University Press, 1995).

Said, Edward, *The End of the Peace Process: Oslo and After* (New York: Pantheon Press, 2000).

Endnotes

1. Bruce Jentleson, *American Foreign Policy: The Dynamics of Choice in the 21st Century* (New York: Norton, 2000), 260.
2. Jentleson, 261.
3. Jentleson, 263.
4. "Wye and the Road to War," Douglas J. Feith, in *Commentary,* January 1999, 43.
5. Feith, 45.
6. William L. Cleveland, *A History of the Modern Middle East* (Boulder, Colo.: Westview Press, 2000), 496.
7. In the presidential campaign of 2000, both George W. Bush and Al Gore had gone to great lengths to proclaim their support for the "special relationship" the United States has with Israel. From the perspective of Palestinians, this raised questions about the ability of the United States to serve as an "honest broker" in negotiations.
8. "Intifada II: Death of an Illusion?" in *Commentary,* December 2000, p. 27.
9. Podhoretz, 36.
10. "Intifada II: The Long Trail of Arab Anti-Semitism," by Efraim Karsh, in *Commentary,* December 2000, 49.
11. Edward W. Said, *The End of the Peace Process: Oslo and After* (New York: Pantheon Books, 2000), xi.
12. Said, xv.
13. Souad Dajani, *Eyes Without Country* (Philadelphia: Temple University Press, 1995), 93.
14. Said, 295.

Selected Bibliography

Abu-Amr, Ziad, *Islamic Fundamentalism in the West Bank and Gaza* (Bloomington: Indiana University Press, 1994).

Abu-Lughod, Ibrahim, *The Arab-Israeli Confrontation of June 1967: An Arab Perspective* (Evanston, IL: Northwestern University Press, 1969).

Amuzegar, Jahangir, *Managing the Oil Wealth: OPEC's Windfalls and Pitfalls* (London: I.B.Tauris, 2001).

Avneri, Arieh, *The Claim of Dispossession: Jewish Land Settlement and the Arabs 1878-1948* (New Brunswick: Transaction Books, 1984).

Baaklini, Abdo, Denoeux, Guilain, and Springborg, Robert, *Legislative Politics in the Arab World: The Resurgence of Democratic Institutions* (Boulder, Colorado: Lynne Rienner, 1999).

Black, C.E., *The Dynamics of Modernization* (New York: Harper and Row, 1966).

Bober, Arie, *The Other Israel: The Radical Case Against Zionism* (New York: Doubleday, 1972).

Bogle, Emory, *The Modern Middle East: From Imperialism to Freedom: 1800-1958* (Upper Saddle River, NJ: Prentice Hall, 1996).

Boorstin, Daniel, *The Image: A Guide to Pseudo-Events in America* (New York: Atheneum, 1971).

Bronner, Stephen, *A Rumor About the Jews: Reflections on Antisemitism and the Protocols of the Learned Elders of Zion* (New York: St. Martin's Press, 2000).

Brown, Carl, *International Politics and the Middle East: Old Rules, Dangerous Game* (Princeton, NJ: Princeton University Press, 1984).

Chafets, Ze'ev, *Double Vision: How the Press Distorts America's View of the Middle East* (New York: William Morrow, 1985).

Chanes, Jerome, *Antisemitism in America* (New York: Carol Publishing Group, 1995).

Chilcote, Ronald, *Theories of Comparative Politics: The Search for a Paradigm Reconsidered* (Boulder, CO: Westview Press, 1994).

Cleveland, William, *A History of the Modern Middle East* (Boulder, Colorado: Westview Press, 2000).

Cohen, Benjamin, *The Question of Imperialism: The Political Economy of Dominance and Dependence* (New York: Basic Books, 1973).

Dajani, Souad, *Eyes Without Country: Searching for a Palestinian Strategy of Liberation* (Philadelphia: Temple University Press, 1995)

Esposito, John, *The Islamic Threat: Myth or Reality* (New York: Oxford University Press, 1992).

Farmanfarmain, Manucher and Roxane, *Blood and Oil: Petroleum Poicymaking in Saudi Arabia* (New York: Modern Library, 1999).

Flapan, Simha, *The Birth of Israel* (New York: Pantheon Books, 1983).

Friedman, Thomas, *From Beirut to Jerusalem* (New York: Anchor Books, 1989).

Gaaklini, Abdo, Denoeux, Guilain, and Robert Springborg, *Legislative Politics in the Arab World* (Boulder, CO: Rienner, 1999).

Ghareeb, Edmund, *Split Vision: The Portrayal of Arabs in the American Media* (Washington, D.C.: American-Arab Affairs Council, 1983).

Goodwin, Jason, *Lords of the Horizons: A History of the Ottoman Empire* (New York: Henry Holt, 1998).

Haj, Samira, *The Making of Iraq 1900-1963: Capital, Power, and Ideology* (Albany: State University of New York Press, 1997).

Hart, Alan, *Arafat* (Bloomington: Indiana University Press, 1984).

Hoffman, Bruce, *Inside Terrorism* (New York: Columbia University Press, 1998).

Jentleson, Bruce, *American Foreign Policy: The Dynamics of Choice in the 21st Century* (New York: Norton, 2000).

Karsh, Efraim and Rautsi, Inari, *Saddam Hussein: A Political Biography* (New York: The Free Press, 1991).

Laqueur, Walter, *The Israel-Arab Reader: A Documentary History of the Middle East Conflict* (New York: Viking Penguin, 1984).

Lenczowski, George, *The Middle East in World Affairs* (Ithaca, NY: Cornell University Press, 1980).

Lester, Paul, *Images that Injure* (Westport, CT: Praeger Publishers, 1996).

Lewis, Bernard, *The Arabs in History* (New York: Oxford University Press, 1994).

———, *The Assassins* (New York: Oxford University Press, 1967).

Mackey, Sandra, *The Iranians* (New York: Plume/Penguin, 1996).

Mishal, Ahaul, and Sela, Avraham, *The Palestinian HAMAS: Vision, Violence, and Coexistence* (New York: Columbia University Press, 2000).

Morris, Benny, *The Birth of the Palestinian Refugee Problem* (Cambridge: Cambridge University Press, 1987).

———, *Righteous Victims: A History of the Zionist-Arab Conflict* (New York: Knopf, 2000).

Obaid, Nawaf, *The Oil Kingdom at 100: Petroleum Policymaking in Saudi Arabia* (Washington, D.C.: The Washington Institute for Near East Policy, 2000).

Parenti, Michael, *Make-Believe Media* (New York: St. Martin's Press, 1992).

Pipes, Daniel, *Greater Syria* (New York: Oxford University Press, 1990).

Prager, Dennis, and Telushkin, Joseph, *Why the Jews: The Reason for Antisemitism* (New York: Simon and Schuster, 1983).

Quandt, William, *Camp David: Peacemaking and Politics* (Washington, D.C.: Brookings Institution, 1986).

Sachar, Howard, *A History of Israel* (New York: Knopf, 1991).

Said, Edward, *The End of the Peace Process: Oslo and After* (New York: Pantheon Press, 2000).

———, *The Question of Palestine* (New York: Vintage Books, 1992).

Shlaim, Avi, *War and Peace in the Middle East* (New York: Penguin, 1995).

Smith, Hedrick, *The Media and the Gulf War* (Washington, D.C.:Seven Locks Press, 1992).

Smith, Jean, *George Bush's War* (New York: Holt, 1992).

Thornton, A.P., *The Imerial Idea and Its Enemies* (New York: Doubleday, 1959).

Wilson, Peter and Graham, Douglas, *Saudi Arabia: The Coming Storm* (Armonk, New York: M.E. Sharpe, 1994).

Zubaida, Sami, *Islam: The People and the State* (New York: I.B. Tauris, 1993).

Index